THE GENTLEMAN SAINT

This book is dedicated with much love to my family

THE GENTLEMAN SAINT

A Pilgrimage to Oxford, Dublin and Rome
in the Footprints of Saint John Henry Newman

Patricia O'Leary

GRACEWING

First published in England in 2020
by
Gracewing
2 Southern Avenue
Leominster
Herefordshire HR6 0QF
United Kingdom
www.gracewing.co.uk

The publishers have no responsibility
for the persistence or accuracy of URLs for websites
referred to in this publication, and do not guarantee
that any content on such websites is, or will remain,
accurate or appropriate.

ISBN 978 085244 760 4

Typeset by Word and Page, Chester, UK

Cover design by Bernardita Peña Hurtado

CONTENTS

Foreword by Dr Patricia Casey ix

Introduction 1

1. A Great English Saint 6

2. London 10

3. A Glance at John Henry Newman's Childhood 22

4. In the Footprints of a Saint 27

5. Annual Pilgrimage to Littlemore 31

6. The Oxford Movement 51

7. Catalogue of the English Saints 55

8. Leaving Littlemore 56

9. Littlemore in the Snow 58

10 Maryvale 59

11. 'Speak I Must' 62

12. Dublin: Newman's Catholic University 66

13. The Discourses: *The Idea of a University* 72

14. Public Lecture at University College Dublin 80

15. To Tervoe for Rest and Silence 82

16. Waiting 84

17. The Second Spring 87

18. A University in Preparation 91

19. A Historic Day: The Opening of Ireland's
    Catholic University 95

20. Dublin University's Collegiate Church,
    Our Lady Seat of Wisdom 100

21. Newman's Prayer Life 105

22. Tributes to University College Dublin's
    First President   108

23. Newman and the Role of the Laity   111

24. Leaving Dublin   115

25. Newman's Legacy to his Dublin University   117

26. Augustine Birrell's Bill of 1908   118

27. Rome   121

28. Rome: Celebration of the Canonization
    of St John Henry Newman   129

29. Evening of Canonization   133

30. Mass of Thanksgiving   135

31. Limerick and Newman   137

32. The *Apologia* is Born   139

33. *The Dream of Gerontius*   143

34. Littlemore College   146

35. The Ordinariate   147

36. The Oxford Newman Society   149

Conclusion   150

Bibliography   155

ACKNOWLEDGEMENTS

In addition to my family, I wish also to acknowledge the help and prayers of:
   The Most Revd Dr Philip Boyce, OCD
   Dr Richard Conrad, OP, Blackfriars, Oxford
   Dr Andrew Nash, Newman scholar—my tutor at Black-friars
   Fr Francis Gavin, Birmingham Oratory
   Dr David Kelly, OSA
   The Sisters of the Work of Christ, Littlemore, Oxford
   Br Aelred, OSB, Pluscarden Abbey

And the 'blessings' in my life:
   My dear friend, Eileen Myers, for her prayers, endless encouragement and generosity
   Cherie O' Sullivan
   Jennifer Moynihan
   Anne, Rosemary, Tony and Clare
   Nigel O'Mahoney, Cork City Library
   Peter and Joyce Clarke, dear friends who first introduced me to Oxford
   Rosemary Walsh, who provided me with a 'home from home' at Oxford
   Melinda, from Budapest, and all my fellow students at Blackfriars
   Rebecka from Sweden, who followed Newman's path to the Catholic Church

I wish also to acknowledge the help of:
   Joey O' Donovan, UCC
   Ms Maureen Quinn, Administrative Officer, UCD
   Ms Eilis O'Brien, Director Communications, UCD

FOREWORD

In writing *The Gentleman Saint*, Patricia O' Leary has done a great service to those who admire Cardinal (now Saint) John Henry Newman, as well as those who simply know the name, but little else about him. A significant part of her book is devoted to his contribution to Irish education. This is as it should be for it is not an exaggeration to say that it was enormous. The impact extended beyond the shores of Ireland, and his series of writings on education and universities, published in book form as *The Idea of a University*, are now a worldwide classic. The Discourses, as they were called, were originally a series of lectures he delivered to the intellectuals of Dublin in 1852 as part of his preparatory work towards establishing a Catholic University in Ireland. Newman himself later admitted that these were the most daunting of any he ever delivered because of the complex of sensitivities he had to face; firstly from Dr Cullen, the archbishop who invited him to assist in establishing the new University, secondly those of the nationalists who might object to a British convert from Oxford having a role, as the University might thus not be properly Irish, and finally the objections of some attendees who felt there was not enough demand for such an institution.

Invited by Archbishop Cullen, the Irish Primate, in 1851 to an Ireland that was just recovering from the famine and only a few decades after Catholic Emancipation was granted, he set about establishing a Catholic University in Ireland, an endeavour that was supported by the Pope. In the course of establishing the University, he criss-crossed the Irish Sea on fifty-six occasions. This book also details his travels around the country, meeting the bishops in order to try and win support for the idea of the university. It was supported by most of them, but as time went on, it appears to have been less enthusiastically received by Archbishop

Cullen himself, who failed to respond to Newman's letters, and also by Bishop Delaney of Cork who favoured the Queen's Colleges which had already been established in Cork and Galway. Despite these travails, his dream was fulfilled and on 3 November 1854 the Catholic University of Ireland was opened at 86 St Stephen's Green.

Newman was responsible for appointing professors from the lay population, as well as some clerics, much to the dismay of the bishops. He established evening lectures for those who were working by day, and allowed students play games, go to the theatre and have social lives. He espoused a liberal education and set up departments of politics and social science, archaeology and theology. He established a chair of poetry and of English Literature and founded what is now known as the Historical and Literary Society, but the jewels in the crown were the opening of the medical school the following year in Earlsfort Terrace and the building of a university church, Our Lady Seat of Wisdom, on St Stephen's Green in a neo-Byzantine style. The project was funded by the laity and received no state grants. He retired from his position as rector and left Ireland for the last time on 4 November 1858. He was later made a Cardinal in 1879 and died in 1890.

In preparing this book Patricia O'Leary immersed herself in Newman's writings, and in his life and times. She lived for a period in Oxford, studying all things relating to Newman and walking the streets that he strode. The result is a sensitive and appreciative appraisal of the work of this great man who last year, on 13 October 2019, was canonised by Pope Francis.

The Catholic University of Ireland ceded its Catholic links in 1908, when the National University of Ireland, was established under the National University of Ireland Act. It became a secular university and this played out in aspects of Newman's canonisation last year. University College Dublin (UCD) and the Government at first declined to send any representative to Rome to celebrate the pinnacle of

Newman's many achievements, in Ireland and on the world stage. The stated reason was that the University was secular. The irony that the future King of England and would-be head of the Church of England was representing the Queen at the occasion and that other secular countries such as France and the USA were being represented may have triggered a moment of insight. Under pressure, that also came from various student and other university groups, both UCD and the Irish State reversed their decision and did send representatives. Nevertheless the initial excuses seem petty and narrow in view of the titanic achievements of Newman in the sphere of University Education. But for the public at large he will be remembered for his defence of Catholicism and for the courageous act of following his conscience to convert to that faith. He is truly deserving of the title Saint John Henry Newman.

Dr Patricia Casey
Professor of Psychiatry, University College Dublin
and Consultant Psychiatrist at the Mater Misericordiae
University Hospital, Dublin

Feast of St John Henry Newman,
9 October 2020

INTRODUCTION

'Academics don't become saints', said John Henry Newman when a friend suggested that he was a saint. I remembered this comment as I looked at the unveiling of the tapestry of this scholarly saint, high on the façade of St Peter's in Rome, in October 2019, announcing to the world that this brilliant scholar of our time is a canonized saint.

I fancied that Newman would have been a little surprised, but also slightly bemused, perhaps, at the idea of being proclaimed a saint of the Universal Church. In addition to his comment above, he often adamantly denied that he had anything of the saint in him, claiming 'I have nothing of a saint about me, as everyone knows, and it is a severe (and salutary) mortification to be thought next door to one ... It is enough for me to black the saints' shoes.'

'There you are', I wanted to shout aloud that morning in Rome, 'Well done, you've made it!'

It is not too big a claim to say that John Henry Newman joins the group of great scholarly saints and doctors of the Church, such as Augustine, Benedict, Thomas Aquinas, Duns Scotus and many more brilliant scholars of other ages, but, importantly, Newman fills this role for our time. He is a saint of our age, with a clear understanding of the problems we face today.

Throughout his writings, for example, he persistently warns of the dangers of the rise of what he terms the 'tyranny of relativism', which is so predominant in today's society. Newman warned of the onslaught of this 'plague', and with the vision of a prophet, he saw how this would come to pass in our age.

This book will aim to 'walk' with John Henry Newman, concentrating primarily on his university years at Oxford, those soul-searching, anxious years of suffering and heart-break before entering the Catholic Church. We will look at what motivated him to give up so much he loved and cared for in order to become a Catholic.

We will then follow him on his many journeys across the Irish Sea, as he took on the mammoth task of setting up a Catholic university in Dublin. Our pilgrim journey will follow Newman's intermittent four journeys to Rome, and look at what was happening in his life at the time of each of these visits to the Eternal City.

We will explore the life of this wonderful saint, and take a cursory look at his childhood and family life.

Newman's whole life was focused on the pursuit of truth. Pope Benedict XVI comments, 'He was a man whose whole life was a journey, a journey in which he allowed himself to be transformed by truth in a search marked by great sincerity and great openness, so as to know better and to find and accept the path that leads to true life'. When Newman, one of the most famous Anglican ministers of the time, converted to Catholicism it is said that 'Victorian England was scandalized'. But our saint had found the truth he was seeking in the Catholic Church and was determined to follow it at whatever cost.

Most people are familiar with at least one of Newman's reflections, for he reaches out to teach and inspire hope and confidence through his beautiful prose and poetry, that touches the deepest yearnings of the human heart in a way few can emulate. As G. K. Chesterton writes:

> The quality of his literary style is so successful that it succeeds in escaping definition. The quality of his logic is that of a long but passionate patience, which waits until he has fixed all corners of an iron trap. But the quality of his moral comment on the age remains what I have said: a protest of the rationality of religion as against the increasing irrationality of mere Victorian comfort and compromise.[1]

Pope Paul IV called Vatican II 'Newman's Council' because so many of his ideas, most particularly the role of the laity, inspired the Council.

We note that liberalism in religion—particularly amongst the clergy—was a lifelong angst for Newman, and learn of his courage and perseverance in persistently speaking out and defending the Church, often at great cost to his own health and welfare.

Newman's primary guides in his search for the truth were his beloved Fathers of the Church, whose lives he explored deeply and methodically, as he explains in his *Apologia*. At a certain point when writing his essay on doctrinal development, he stopped, having read the words of Augustine, leaving the thesis incomplete. He had found the truth he was searching for in the Catholic Church and decided at that point to enter what he termed 'the one fold of Christ'.

Even though he was a brilliant scholar, Newman was a very humble man who has become a saint because of his holiness of life, his great kindness and compassion and goodness to the poor and those in need.

Of his gifted preaching, Bishop Boyce writes, 'In the pulpit he gave the impression of meditating with his God and of drawing his audience along with him'.

Another writer describes the 'prayerfulness' of Newman's preaching as follows: 'The look and bearing of the preacher were as of one who dwelt apart, who, though he knew his age well, did not live in it ... he seemed to come forth that one day of the week (Sunday) to speak to others of the things he had seen and known'. Beauty, Truth and Goodness were thus the aim of Cardinal Newman's life, and these three transcendentals represent his pilgrimage to the sainthood of the Catholic Church, through a life in search for the one who is Beauty, Truth and Goodness.

Cardinal Newman advises what to look for in the life of a saint—not suspecting for a moment that he would be giving advice as to what to look for in his own life:

> A saint's writings are to me his real 'Life'. Commonly, what is called 'the Life' is little more than a collection of anecdotes brought together from a number of

3

independent quarters; anecdotes striking, indeed, and
edifying, but valuable in themselves rather than valuable
as parts of a biography; valuable whoever was the subject
of them, not valuable as illustrating a particular saint.[2]

When he was created cardinal in 1879, he took his motto,
'Heart speaks to heart', from a letter by Francis de Sales. But
Newman's words do indeed speak to the heart—it would
be impossible to find words to convey the sentiments of the
human heart with such beauty and sensitivity.

As to his personality, his biographer, Ian Ker, notes,
'Newman was a person of great charm, compassion and
kindness. He had a great sense of humour like St Thomas
More. He also had a great gift for friendship.' The travel
writer Douglas Sladen, who occupied Newman's old rooms
at Oriel, and who met the newly elected cardinal on his visit
to Oxford in 1880, describes him as follows: 'A wan little
old man with a shrivelled face and a large nose, and one
of the most beautiful expressions which ever appeared on
a human being'.[3]

This book is dedicated to using Newman's own words
and phrases as much as possible in the certain belief that
this is how we can learn from his life and how England's
new saint would wish his many teachings to be relayed.

In our day a dictatorship of a false ideology is imposed
on young people, and a culture of consumerism pressures
them in relation as to what to wear how to think and behave
in the name of being 'cool' at all costs. Sadly, the youth of
today have become cynical of a world with an economy of
truth, that is more interested in profit than people.

St John Henry Newman always pointed to the hope that
is always available to us, as he leads the way to the truth that
every human being was made for and on to the dawning
of that 'Second Spring' that with the vision of a prophet he
predicts for the Church and for society.

Notes

[1] G. K. Chesterton, *The Victorian Age in Literature*, London, H. Holt & Co, 1913, ch. 1.

[2] Newman, *Historical Sketches*, vol. 2.

[3] I. Ker, *John Henry Newman, A Biography*, Oxford: Oxford University Press, 1990, p. 726.

A Great English Saint for Our Times

S T John Henry Newman, who was canonized in Rome on 13 October 2019, is the first English person to become a saint since Reformation times.

But London-born John Henry Newman—a former Anglican clergyman who converted to Catholicism and became a Roman Catholic priest—is the first English saint who was not a martyr since medieval times.

The enormous significance of the sainthood of this English Oratorian priest, best known as 'Cardinal Newman', and its ground-breaking impact for the Catholic Church in England—the people of Newman's own 'dear country'—and for the worldwide Church, will take some time to be fully appreciated.

While he was talented in so many areas of scholarship, it is the uniquely beautiful style of his prose and poetry that is arguably John Henry Newman's greatest gift of all to a world in need of the hope, sensitivity and encouragement he induces through his writing. As Cardinal Cahal B. Daly notes,

> Newman is undeniably one of the great writers and stylists of all time, an incomparable master of the English language, whether spoken or written, but also one in whose writings the man himself becomes present as a warm, sensitive, loving, and above all intensely human personality.[1]

As a brilliant scholar, theologian, philosopher and educator, he ranks amongst the great intellectual saints and

doctors of the Church. Thus Newman's canonization is celebrated in universities throughout the Catholic and Anglican
world, particularly at the two universities he was personally
involved with.

At Oxford University, his beloved Alma Mater, which
was his home as an undergraduate and later as an eminent academic for almost thirty years, St John Henry
Newman now joins the list of twenty saints of the alumni
of the university. Most of these saints were Reformation
martyrs put to death for their Catholic faith between 1535
and 1642, the best known of whom are St Thomas More
and St Edmund Campion.

The Catholic University Newman founded in Dublin—
the present University College Dublin—now has the rare
distinction that its founder and first president is a saint. This
places Ireland's largest university in the unique position of
having its founder numbered amongst the extremely rare
group of scholar-saints to have founded universities and
monastic institutions throughout the centuries.

Who could have foreseen that when John Henry Newman crossed the Irish Sea in 1851 to a country he knew
little or nothing about, in order to take on the onerous task
of setting up a Catholic university in Dublin, the unique
university he founded with so much care and diligence on
Irish soil in those difficult post-Famine years would grow
into Ireland's largest university today. 'It is plain every great
change is effected by the few, not by the many; by the reso-
lute, undaunted, zealous few.'[2]

But Newman was a visionary, as we see in the following
beautiful address delivered by the founder and first president of the Catholic University, on the day it opened its
doors on the feast of the great Irish saint Malachy in 1854. In
this hope-filled address, Newman, with a prophetic vision,
pointed to the 'brighter day' and the flourishing university
that has indeed come to pass:

> I look towards a land both old and young; old in its
> Christianity, young in the promise of its future ... I

7

contemplate a people which has had a long night, and will have an inevitable day. I am turning my eyes towards a hundred years to come, and I dimly see the island I am gazing on become the road of passage and union between two hemispheres, and the centre of the world ... The capital of that prosperous and hopeful land is situate in a beautiful bay and near a romantic region; and in it I see a flourishing university, which for a while had to struggle with fortune, but which, when its first founders and servants were dead and gone, had successes far exceeding their anxieties.[3]

The beautiful University Church of Our Lady Seat of Wisdom that Newman founded on St Stephen's Green in Dublin stands today as a further tribute to this scholarly saint's legacy to his Dublin university and to the people of Ireland.

The reason I refer to John Henry Newman as 'the gentleman saint' is that, as we will see throughout this book, the characteristics of the 'gentleman' are very important to Newman and are qualities that this saint embodies. He wants the students at his university to be 'gentlemen', which is something, he asserts, that 'I shall illustrate and insist upon'.[4] But, in addition to all these worthy qualities, Newman's 'gentleman' will have God in his life. For Newman education is about forming the whole person, morally as well as intellectually, hence the importance of the teaching of theology at his Catholic university.

The following is taken from Newman's renowned definition of a gentleman:

It is almost a definition of a gentleman to say that he is one who never inflicts pain. He is mainly occupied in merely removing the obstacles which hinder the free and unembarrassed action of those about him; and he concurs with their movements rather than take the initiative himself ... The true gentleman ... carefully avoids whatever may cause a jar or a jolt in the minds of those with whom he is cast ... his great concern being to make everyone at his ease and at home ... He has too much good sense to be affronted at insults, he is too well employed to remember injuries, and too indolent to bear malice . . . Nowhere shall we find greater candour, consideration, indulgence: he throws himself into the minds of his opponents, he accounts for their mistakes. He knows the weakness of human reason as well as its strength, its province and its limits.[5]

Newman's brilliant classic, *The Idea of a University*, which is the accumulation of his discourses—'well-thought ideas' for his Dublin university—is said to 'rank among the masterpieces of the English language',[6] whilst a further citation by Sir Arthur Quiller-Couch, one of England's best-known *literati* of the twentieth century, claims 'This book is so wise—so eminently wise as to deserve being bound by the young student of literature for a frontlet on his brow and as a talisman on his writing wrist'.[7]

Notes

[1] Cardinal Cahal B. Daly, *Blessed John Henry Newman: His Relevance for Today*, Lecture given at Cardinal Tomás Ó Fiaich Memorial Library and Archive, 2006. Armagh: Cumann Seanchais Ard Mhacha, 2010, p. 22.

[2] Newman, *Parochial and Plain Sermons*.

[3] D. McCartney, *UCD: A National Idea: The History of University College Dublin*, Dublin: Gill & Macmillan, 1999, p. 12.

[4] Newman, *The Idea of a University*.

[5] *Ibid.*

[6] Newman, *The Idea of a University; Defined and Illustrated*, ed. D. M. O'Connell, Chicago: Loyola University Press, 1927, Introduction, p. x.

[7] Sir Arthur Quller-Couch, *On the Art of Writing*, Lectures delivered to the University of Cambridge, 1913–14, Cambridge: Cambridge University Press, 1916, p. 27.

✝ 2 ✝

London

'BLESSINGS'—NEWMAN'S FRIENDS

C ARDINAL NEWMAN counted his friends as 'blessings' in his life, and indeed the mounting list of these 'blessings' continues to grow, as more and more people are learning to appreciate the rich legacy he has left through his writings and teaching. 'Blessings of friends, which to my door unasked, unhoped, have come. They have come, they have gone; they came to my great joy, they went to my great grief'.[1]

One of Newman's faithful friends—who as a young seminarian had come to appreciate John Henry's teaching on conscience many years ago—Pope Benedict XVI—decided to travel especially to Britain for Newman's beatification ceremony in September 2010.

Pope Benedict paid Cardinal Newman a huge honour by travelling to Britain for the event. Previously this Pontiff had not attended beatification ceremonies and never before had a beatification ceremony been held in England. But Pope Benedict greatly revered the English cardinal and wanted to honour this extraordinary churchman in his own 'beloved country' and among his own people, as he firmly believed Newman would have wished.

So on a beautiful, sunny autumn day on 18 September 2010, I joined the large crowd outside Westminster Cathedral waiting for Pope Benedict XVI to emerge after a special celebratory Mass in honour of Cardinal Newman. The beatification ceremony was due to take place in Birmingham the following day.

The then Archbishop Vincent Nichols of Westminster (now cardinal), together with the bishops of England and Wales, heads of other churches and some 250 priests and dignities from all branches of public and political life filled the cathedral to capacity that morning. The Pontiff singled out the Anglican Archbishop of Canterbury, Dr Rowan Williams, for a special greeting when he told the congregation: 'In a particular way I greet the Archbishop of Canterbury, who honours us by his presence', recognizing, of course, that Cardinal Newman is also revered by Anglicans.

The large crowd gathered outside Westminster Cathedral stretched back as far as the eye could see. Amongst this group were some 2,500 young people from dioceses throughout the United Kingdom, who radiated a lively sense of warmth and exuberance, obviously delighted to be present for this historic occasion of the first state visit of a pope to England, and here specially to honour their own beloved, and soon to become 'blessed', John Henry Newman.

After Mass, Pope Benedict came and stood outside the cathedral, smiling warmly as the young people cheered and clapped, and chanted their famous affectionate 'clarion call' chosen for this popular Pontiff at all youth gatherings: 'Benedetto, Benedetto'.

The Pontiff told the exuberant crowd that he chose Cardinal Newman's motto, 'Heart speaks to heart' — *Cor ad cor loquitur* — as the theme of his visit.

It was wonderful to be in London on that historic day and to personally witness the transformation of that great city, where the 'aggressive secularism' that Pope Benedict spoke about on his arrival in Britain could generally be said to abound. But on that special day — appropriately bathed in brilliant sunshine to welcome its distinguished guest — London took on the aura of a large village where perfect strangers became neighbours, sharing banter and good cheer with one another. Despite predictions to the contrary beforehand, the media had given kind and gracious coverage to Pope Benedict's visit since his arrival in the country, treating him with the utmost courtesy and respect. 'Gentle and full of compassion', were the terms mostly used by the BBC to describe Pope Benedict XVI.

Soon the group around me began winding their way towards Hyde Park for a long five-hour wait before the prayer vigil in preparation for Cardinal Newman's beatification the following day in Birmingham was due to begin. As the afternoon progressed, more and more people joined the moving stream negotiating their way through London's bustling Saturday-afternoon shoppers, many of whom stood awe-struck at the long winding river of people commandeering the capital's busy streets.

Cardinal Newman's many friends and devotees had travelled from all over the United Kingdom, Ireland, the Continent, the United States and numerous parts of the world for this historic event in honour of their much-loved 'English gentleman' cardinal.

One certainly sensed Newman's spirit infiltrating his native city that day in the abundant joy that prevailed. There were no solemn litanies or hymn singing—that would come later. First, people wanted to share the joy and appreciation of this wonderful event that so many had consistently prayed for, over many, many years.

The jubilant atmosphere brought to mind a sense of Newman's 'Second Spring' whereby this prophetic scholarly saint foresaw the dawning of 'the resurrection of the Church' in England:

> We are engaged in a great, a joyful work ... but expect trials and sufferings, for 'to set up the Church again in England is too great an act to be done in a corner. We have had reason to expect that such a boon would not be given to us without a cross. It is not God's way that great blessings should descend without the sacrifice first of great sufferings.[2]

THE CHURCH IN TEARS

These self-same streets had witnessed much suffering and barbarism during Reformation times, when so many martyrs were dragged along, chained and shackled, before being hung, drawn and quartered on Tyburn Hill for their Catholic faith:[3] 'The long imprisonment, the fetid dungeon, the weary suspense, the tyrannous trial, the barbarous sentence, the savage execution, the rack, the gibbet, the knife, the cauldron, the numberless tortures of those holy victims'.[4]

With the dissolution of the monasteries, precious religious objects and ancient books were brought to this place of execution in London to be publicly desecrated and burned, including the precious statue of Our Lady of Walsingham, from the national shrine to Our Lady in Norfolk. For centuries, after their coronation, England's monarchs had walked the holy mile to this shrine to honour the Queen of Heaven and seek her help and protection for their people.

Courageous saints such as St Thomas More, executed on Tower Hill, and a myriad of martyrs — among them some thirteen saints and many more blesseds from Oxford University — who stood firmly in defence of their Catholic faith when the world around them had gone mad — set the seed for the dawning of this special day. The courageous Londoner who was being honoured here had also endured great suffering because of his decision to enter his beloved Catholic Church, which he called 'the one fold of Christ'.

JOY PREDOMINATES IN LONDON

Yet this was a joyous occasion, a special day when this city was celebrating the life of an 'exemplary' Londoner, one of their own, who had dug deep into his Christian roots and brought to light the truth of the faith that for centuries had been loved and practised by the people of a country that had once been known by the precious title 'the Dowry of

Mary' — a country whose kings and queens have been exemplary models of the Christian faith for their people throughout many centuries, as the present monarch has shown.

When I saw the huge stream of people fill the pavements of this secular city to overflowing as they walked purposely towards Hyde Park on that sunny September day I realized the wisdom of Pope Benedict's decision in travelling to Britain for Newman's beatification. For an air of joy and sheer delight was clearly evident amongst the surging throng of people, all here to celebrate this, their own day, when a pope from Rome had come to honour a son of this great city.

Queen Elizabeth II had issued an official invitation to Pope Benedict XVI; this was the first state visit of a pope to the United Kingdom (Pope John Paul II's visit in 1982, though he did meet the Queen, was a pastoral rather than state visit). As a guest of the Queen, Pope Benedict came as a visitor to all the people of the United Kingdom — not just the Catholic population — to preside over the beatification of John Henry Newman. During his visit the Pontiff also took part in many ecumenical and inter-religious services.

On this historic day London was witnessing a new dawn for Catholics and Anglicans alike. For all of this came about because one of this city's own, a former Anglican minister revered by both Catholics and Anglicans, was to be beatified, the last step on the road to sainthood.

WESTMINSTER HALL ADDRESS

In his Westminster Hall address to an audience that included four former prime ministers and hundreds of members of 'civil society' Pope Benedict paid homage to the courage and tenacity of the much-loved, London-born, St Thomas More. 'The great English scholar and statesman, who is so admired by believers and non-believers alike for the integrity with which he followed his conscience, even at the cost of displeasing the sovereign whose "good servant" he was, because he chose to serve God first.'[5]

Pope Benedict was not lacking in courage, either, as he spoke of the threat posed to society by 'aggressive secularism', a concern also echoed by the Archbishop of Canterbury and the Chief Rabbi during the visit. The Pontiff also decried the politically correct idea that Christmas should not be celebrated for fear of offending minorities. Praising those politicians who took it upon themselves to fight for religious respect and dialogue, he stressed that

> the total exclusion of religion from public debate could leave reason and ideology vulnerable to distortions that fail to take full account of the dignity of each individual. I cannot but voice my concern at the increasing marginalization of religion, particularly of Christianity, that is taking place in some quarters, even in nations which place a great emphasis on tolerance. . . There are those who would advocate that the voice of religion be silenced, or at least relegated to the purely private sphere.

Cardinal Newman had witnessed the first cycle of the state's attempts to 'silence' the voice of religion during his Oxford days of the 1820s and 1830s, when no more pupils were allotted to him at Oriel because of his concern for their spiritual values. Pope Benedict had also suffered greatly from the totalitarian regime he had witnessed during his childhood in Germany and as a seminarian at Freising University. 'The unity of the Church Catholic is very near my heart, only I do not see any prospect of it in our time, and I despair of its being effected without great sacrifices on all hands'.[6]

At Lambeth Palace Pope Benedict, addressing the Archbishop of Canterbury, paid homage to Cardinal Newman's Anglican background:

> In the figure of John Henry Newman . . . we celebrate a churchman whose ecclesial vision was nurtured by his Anglican background and matured during his many years of ordained ministry in the Church of England.

He can teach us the virtues that ecumenism demands; on the one hand, he was moved to follow his conscience, even at great personal cost; and on the other hand, the warmth of his continued friendship with his former colleagues led him to explore with them, in a truly eirenical spirit, the questions on which they differed, driven by a deep longing for unity in faith.

The historic image of the Roman Catholic Pontiff with the leader of the Anglican Church kneeling in prayer before the tomb of St Edward the Confessor at Westminster Abbey, paying tribute to Newman's Anglican and Roman Catholic heritage, would delight the heart of England's new saint, who worked so tirelessly for Christian unity in his lifetime. It is an iconic vision to be treasured.

And I earnestly pray for this whole company, with a hope against hope, that all of us, who once were so united, and so happy in our union, may even now be brought at length, by the Power of the Divine Will, into One Fold and under One Shepherd.[7]

THE SUN SETS OVER LONDON

As the sun set over London that September evening some 80,000 people gathered to pray and to reflect on the life of the city's new 'blessed', led by Pope Benedict, who celebrated the prayer vigil in preparation for the beatification ceremony the following day in Birmingham. Addressing the crowd the Pope explained that Cardinal Newman's beatification was a great personal joy for him, as Newman had long been an important influence in his own life and thought since his days as a seminarian at university.

During his four-day visit Pope Benedict offered many insights into the life of this 'exemplary figure'. But the crucial message, often aired by him was to warn against the dangers of the 'aggressive secularism' prevalent throughout Britain.

In our day, when an intellectual and moral relativism threatens to sap the very foundations of our society, Newman reminds us that, as men and women made in the image and likeness of God, we were created to know the truth, to find in that truth our ultimate freedom and the fulfilment of our deepest human aspirations. In a word, we were meant to know Christ, who is himself 'the way, and the truth, and the life' (John 14:6).[8]

The Pontiff further stressed that Newman's life also teaches us that 'passion for the truth; intellectual honesty and genuine conversion are costly. The truth that sets us free cannot be kept to ourselves, it calls for testimony, it begs to be heard, and in the end its convincing power comes from itself and not from the human eloquence or arguments in which it may be couched.'

Not far from Hyde Park at Tyburn Hill great numbers of our 'brothers and sisters' had died for the faith;

the witness of their fidelity to the end was ever more powerful than the inspired words that so many of them spoke before surrendering everything to the Lord. In our own time, the price to be paid for fidelity to the Gospel is no longer being hanged, drawn and quartered but it often involves being dismissed out of hand, ridiculed or parodied.

Pope Benedict further attested:

Newman taught that the 'kindly light' of faith leads us to realize the truth about ourselves, our dignity as God's children, and the sublime destiny which awaits us in heaven. By letting the light of faith shine in our hearts, and by abiding in that light through our daily union with the Lord in prayer and participation in the life-giving sacraments of the Church, we ourselves become light to those around us; we exercise our 'prophetic office', often, without even knowing it, we draw people one step closer to the Lord and his truth ... without the life of prayer, without the interior transformation which takes place through the grace of the sacraments, we cannot, in Newman's words, 'radiate Christ'; we become just another 'clashing cymbal' (1 Cor 13:1) in a world filled with growing noise and confusion, filled with false paths leading only to heart-break and illusion.

Pope Benedict said that God has always raised up great saints and prophets for the renewal of the Church and Christian society in times of crisis and upheaval. But there is personal responsibility, as Newman believed; 'each of us has a mission to change the world, to work for a culture of life, a culture forged by love and respect for the dignity of each human person' (Pope Benedict).

Cardinal Newman's much-loved reflection, that has been an inspiration for so many people to ponder and reflect on the meaning of life, was then quoted by Pope Benedict:

> God has created me to do him some definite service. He has committed some work to me which he has not committed to another. I have my mission. I may never know it in this world. But I shall be told it in the next. I am a link in the chain, a bond of connection between persons. He has not created me for naught. I shall do good. I shall do his work. I shall be an angel of peace. A preacher of truth in my own place, while not intending it. If I do but keep his commandments. Therefore, I will trust him. Wherever, whatever I am, I can never be thrown away. If I am in sickness, my sickness may serve him; in perplexity, my perplexity may serve him; if I am in sorrow, my sorrow may serve him. He does nothing in vain. He knows what he is about. He may take away my friends, he may throw me among strangers. He may make me feel desolate, make my spirits sink, hide my future from me ... still ... he knows what he is about.[9]

As that historic day drew to a close, it was time for private prayer and reflection before the Blessed Sacrament; 'Christ, present among us. In a special way, let us thank Him for the enduring witness to the truth offered by Cardinal John Henry Newman. Trusting in his prayers, let us ask the Lord to illumine our path, and the path of all British society, with the "kindly light" of his truth, his love and his peace', Pope Benedict declared.

The vigil concluded with Newman's poetic words set to music in that beautiful hymn 'Lead, Kindly Light'. And a multitude of voices, in rapturous unison, sent Cardinal Newman's encouraging message of Christ's enduring love and protection for each one of us amid the storms of life, out across the rooftops of this great city, and further afield above the bridges and barges of the Thames.

> *Lead, Kindly Light, amid the encircling gloom,*
>   *lead Thou me on!*
> *The night is dark, and I am far from home –*
>   *lead Thou me on!*
> *Keep Thou my feet; I do not ask to see*
> *The distant scene—one step enough for me.*
>
> *I was not ever thus, nor prayed that Thou*
>   *should'st lead me on;*
> *I loved to choose and see my path; but now*
>   *lead Thou me on!*
> *I loved the garish day, and, spite of fears,*
> *Pride ruled my will. Remember not past years!*
>
> *So long Thy power hath blest me sure it still*
>   *will lead me on.*
> *O'er moor and fen, o'er crag and torrent, till*
>   *the night is gone,*
> *And with the morn those angel faces smile, which I*
> *Have loved long since, and lost awhile!*

FAREWELL TO LONDON

Before bidding farewell to London I recalled the words of F. W. Faber—Newman's fellow Oratorian and Oxford convert—and the contribution he made to the much-loved London Oratory.

When Cardinal Newman and his friends were at Maryville they were joined by Frederick Faber—a poet and devotional writer of note—and another group of converts. Fr Faber's group held Newman in very high esteem, but they wanted to adopt a triumphalist approach that would loudly announce that the Catholic Church was once again alive in England. But Newman disliked this approach, believing that with anti-Catholic prejudices being so strong at that time such methods would be counter-productive and draw further ire against the Church and the Catholic population. 'In presenting and defending the truth, Newman was always careful to find the appropriate language, the right form and appropriate tone. He sought not ever to offend and to render testimony to the gentle inner light (kindly light), making an effort to convince with humility, joy and patience.'[10] It was agreed that Faber and his group should move to the London Oratory, which was established on 31 May 1849. And so when Cardinal Newman established the Oratory in Birmingham, Faber became head of the London Community, founded first in King William Street off the Strand (and now named King William IV Street), and then at Brompton. Faber, who became known as 'the parish priest of London', wrote some 150 much-loved hymns, including 'Faith of Our Fathers' in honour of the Reformation martyrs and 'Sweet Star of the Sea'. In these we see a sense of the wealth of the Anglican contribution to the music of the Catholic liturgy.

Fr Faber writes of London:

> How one comes to love this great huge London, when God has thrown us into it as our vineyard! The monster— it looks so unmanageable, and it is positively so awfully wicked, so hopelessly magnificent, so heretically wise and proud after its own fashion. Yet after a fashion it is good also. Such a multitudinous remnant who have never bowed the knee to Baal, such numbers seeking their way to the light, such hearts Grace touched, so much secret holiness, such supernatural lives, such loyalty, mercy, sacrifice, sweetness, greatness. St Vincent Ferrer preached in its streets, and Fr Colombiere in its mews. Do not keep down what is good in it. Help people to be saints. Not all who ask for help really wish it, when it comes to be painful. But some do. Raise ten

souls to detachment from creatures, and to close union with God, and what will happen to this monster city? Who can tell? Poor Babylon! would she might have a blessing from her unknown God, and that Grace might find its way even into her Areopagus![11]

Newman admitted that Faber was a good priest and brought many converts into the Church, but he did cause Cardinal Newman—in his role as founder and head of the English Oratorians—a great deal of stress and anxiety.

May my countenance always be open and joyful, and my words gentle and pleasing, as is suitable for those who, no matter what the state of their life, enjoy the greatest of all goods, the favour of God and the expectation of eternal happiness.[12]

Notes

[1]   Newman, *Apologia.*

[2]   Newman, 'Second Spring'.

[3]   A crypt dedicated to the Reformation martyrs forms an essential part of the convent that stands at Tyburn today. The last of these martyrs to die at Tyburn was the Irish primate, St Oliver Plunkett.

[4]   Newman, 'Second Spring'.

[5]   Westminster Hall Address in *The Daily Telegraph,* 18 Sept. 2010.

[6]   Newman, *Apologia.*

[7]   *Ibid.*

[8]   Address at Hyde Park, 18 Sept. 2010.

[9]   Newman, *Meditations of the Late Cardinal Newman,* London: Longmans, Green & Co., 1907, p. 301.

[10] Paper presented by Pope Benedict at a Newman conference in Rome, November 2010; J. H. Newman, *Meditations and Prayers,* Milan, 2002, pp. 193–4.

[11] F. W. Faber, *Growth in Holiness. The Progress of the Spiritual Life,* London, 1855.

[12] Newman, prayer addressed to St Philip Neri.

✢ 3 ✢

A Glance at Newman's Childhood

J OHN HENRY NEWMAN was born in London on Satur-
day, 21 February 1801, at 80 Old Broad Street, the eldest
son of John Newman, a London banker, and Jemima
Fourdrinier of French Huguenot heritage. The couple, who
married in 1799, had six children, three boys and three girls,
of whom John Henry was the eldest and the undoubted
favourite. Newman and his siblings thrived in this close,
loving family.

They were comfortably off and as the family grew they
moved to a larger house at 17 Southampton Street, Blooms-
bury, in 1802. They also acquired a country house, Grey
Court House, near Ham Common, which had a small farm
attached where they kept many beloved pet animals. Newman and his siblings spent three idyllic summers of their
childhood at this house.

In later years Newman spoke of the happy times they
spent at Grey Court House and how he loved this house
more than any other. When he visited it fifteen years after
they had left, he found the experience very painful.

Newman had been brought up in the Church of England. His parents belonged to what Newman later called
'the national religion of England' or 'Bible religion', which
'consists, not in rites or creeds, but mainly in having the
Bible read in church, in the family, and in private'.[1]

We see the little John Henry sitting with his grandmother—his father's mother—at her house at Fulham
and she is reading to him from the Bible. He lives for long

periods at her house. It is thought this was during the births of his siblings at home, which would have been common practice in those days. 'I was brought up from a child to take a great delight in reading the Bible; but I had no formed religious convictions till I was fifteen. Of course I had a perfect knowledge of my Catechism.'[2]

On 1 May 1808, at the age of seven, John Henry was sent to a private boarding school at Ealing. The reason his father sent him off to school at such a young age was because he was extremely bright and intelligent, so it seemed the right thing to do for him. Small for his age and of slight build, John Henry is described as 'only a babe' when hurdled into this world of burlier, older boys.

The seven-year-old was found in tears by the headmaster, Dr Nicholas, after his parents had left following their first visit. Through sobs, little John Henry, who couldn't stop crying, claimed the boys in the Common Room on the other side of the door would tease him and say 'dreadful things' when they saw he was crying. Dr Nicholas assured him that of course they would not tease him, but the little boy persisted: 'O Sir, they will say such things! I can't help crying … Come and see for yourself!'[3] Taking the master's hand the little boy insists that he bring him into the room. Afterwards there was never a problem with the other boys. But there never was any question of bullying at the Ealing School. In fact later on when his father proposed sending him to another school that he thought might be better suited to John Henry's intellectual capabilities, he didn't want to leave.

Newman is remembered as a charming, cheerful, witty and brilliant young boy who took part in many school activities, such as school plays, and was much liked by the other boys. He soon mastered Latin and Greek and moved up the school system with great speed. He also learned to play his beloved violin at an early age. His gift as a writer and an orator became evident in those early school years, when he won prizes for speeches and wrote a magazine called 'The Spy' and a second paper called 'The Anti-Spy'.

MUSICAL FAMILY

All the family were musical. John Henry's grandfather, John Newman, is described in a pedigree as 'Citizen and Musician', and a member of the Worshipful Company of Musicians. John Henry became so proficient on the violin, Tom Mozley notes; 'had he not become a Doctor of the Church, he would have been a Paganini'.[4]

The Power of Music

Music's ethereal power was given
Not to dissolve our clay,
But draw Promethean beams from heaven
To purge and dross away.

CHANGE IN THE FAMILY'S' CIRCUMSTANCES

The events of 8 March 1816 changed the circumstances of the Newman family radically, when as a result of a financial crisis, the father's bank failed. Consequently, the house in Southampton Street had to be let and their beloved Vine Cottage at Norwood was sold. That summer the three girls were sent to live with their grandmother and aunt until the autumn, when the family moved to 59 High Street, Alton, Hampshire.

Thanks to his partners in the bank, John Newman got a job as manager of a brewery in Alton. Being very principled people, John and his wife saw to it that the creditors were all paid in full, but their changed circumstances were a heart-wrenching experience for all the family.

We find the sensitive John Henry particularly devastated when he was called back from school to hear the news, aged fifteen. His mother wrote, 'I am anxious to know how the dear fellow feels and I trust to be able to soften any keen feelings he may have'.[5]

That same summer of 1816 Newman suffered what he termed the first of the 'three great illnesses' of his life. 'This first keen, terrible one, when I was a boy of 15, made me a Christian with experiences before and after, awful and known only to God.'[6] Because of this illness and the circumstances at home he had to remain at school throughout the summer holidays, where he came under the influence of an evangelical teacher, Walter Mayers. As a result of this encounter Newman underwent what he later termed 'a conversion', the result of which was that he came to a personal belief in God and of a definite creed. He believed that God had some special task for him to accomplish and that he was to live a celibate life to be fully available for this task which God would show him. He writes in his *Apologia*: 'When I was fifteen (in the autumn of 1816), a great change of thought took place in me. I fell under the influences of a definite creed, and received into my intellect impressions of dogma, which, through God's mercy, have never been effaced or obscured'.[7]

When John Newman's job at the brewery in Alton came to an end the family returned to London and to their house in Southampton Street. John Newman continued in the same line of work as a brewer in Clerkenwell, but in 1821 disaster struck and on 1 November he was declared bankrupt—in the Commission of Bankruptcy he is described as a 'Brewer, Dealer and Chapman'.

NEWMAN, A GREAT ENCOURAGER

Newman was a great encourager: we note this over and over again throughout his writings. In a letter to his mother at this time, he wrote: 'When I look around I see few families but what are disturbed from within ... we have not had to weep over the death of those we love ... There is nothing in any way to fear ... All things work together for good to those who love God.'[8] The public exposure in the press triggered by his father's bankruptcy was extremely difficult for all the family.

Five years after being summoned from his school at Ealing, John Henry was called back from Oxford to discuss the latest family financial crisis. His father advised him 'the ship was sinking' and that he had better take back to Oxford any little treasures he especially cherished. But he did not, and was sorry afterwards.

The bankruptcy proceedings dragged on for almost a year. A particularly poignant and embarrassing notice in the *London Gazette* on 21 May 1822 desired his father's creditors 'to meet at the Court of Commissioners of Bankrupts, in Basinghall-Street, in the City of London, to assent to or dissent from the Assignees restoring the trinkets of the Bankrupt's wife taken under the said Commission [of bankruptcy]'.[9]

It is not known whether Mrs Newman's 'trinkets', which were obviously just of sentimental value as everything of value had been sold, were indeed restored to her.

Afterwards John Henry's parents and the two younger children went to live in rented accommodation at Kentish Town Terrace; by 1824 they had moved to York Street, Covent Garden, where they lived very frugally until John Newman's death in September 1824.[10]

Notes

[1] Newman, *An Essay in Aid of a Grammar of Assent*, p. 43.
[2] M. Ward, *Young Mr. Newman*, London: Sheed & Ward, 1948, p. 23.
[3] *Ibid.*, p. 4.
[4] *Ibid.*, p. 11.
[5] S. O'Faolain, *Newman's Way*, London: Longmans, Green and Co., 1952.
[6] Newman, *Autobiographical Writings*, p. 150.
[7] *Ibid.*, p. 169.
[8] O'Faolain, *Newman's Way*, p. 67.
[9] *The London Gazette*, no. 17819 (21 May 1822), p. 856.
[10] O'Faolain, *Newman's Way*, p. 69.

In the Footprints of a Saint

There's a saint in that man
Bishop Ullathorne

I N ORDER TO LEARN MORE about the saints we are curious to visit the places associated with them—the ground on which they walked—in a bid to get to know them better and feel closer to them. That September day in London prompted my decision to learn more about this extraordinary saint, who committed his life to searching for the truth and to the work he believed that God wanted him to do.

And so I decided, firstly, to visit Oxford, the city so beloved of Newman, where he spent so many memorable years of his life. My quest was to learn what motivates a crowd of two hundred thousand, and hundreds of thousands more throughout the world, to follow this humble, gentle saintly academic.

UP TO OXFORD

Later in the autumn of 2010 I was on my way to Oxford. The ancient city that had been our saint's home for almost thirty years of his life was surely the place to begin my journey in his footsteps.

My first impression of beautiful Oxford was of a place caught in a more gracious, more gentle age. It was like stepping back in time or emerging from the wardrobe of C. S. Lewis's Narnia onto a mystical world of enchanting beauty and wonder; of cobbled streets with carefully preserved traditional shop fronts and ancient golden Cotswold stone buildings, with those gracious 'dreaming spires' adding a surreal quality to the beauty of this gracious city.

The lantern-style street lamps—similar to the gas lamps of old—evoked the idea that one could expect to see the lamp-lighter of old moving along in the stillness of the darkened evenings. I begin to see how the sensitive, poetic Newman would love Oxford and how it would be easy to enter into his story here.

I arrived when this ancient city and its surrounds was festooned with the beauty of autumn shades and colours and had the joy of experiencing the sight of the shrubs and trees of Christ Church meadow—where Newman so often took his daily walk—sculptured in the frost and snow of winter and bedecked with the fresh buds of spring, thus moving from the death and decay of autumn to the birth of new life and all the joys of springtime.

THE BELLS OF OXFORD

The bells of Oxford make an important contribution to this ancient city. Newman speaks of the effect that the Church bells had on him:

> Bells pealing. The pleasure of hearing them. It leads the mind to a longing after something I know not what. It does not bring past years to remembrance. It does not bring anything. What does it do? I have a kind of longing after something dear to us and well known to us, very soothing. Such is my feeling at this minute, as I hear them.[1]

But there was a very joyous occasion when the Oxford bells rang out from three towers especially for Newman. The occasion was to congratulate him on becoming a Fellow of Oriel College.

In the Footprints of a Saint

BLACKFRIARS HALL

As a studium student at Blackfriars Hall, I was introduced to the daily round of lectures, study and the discipline of preparing essays for my tutor, as Newman would have done—at a much more advanced level I hasten to add—as an undergraduate. We learn that Newman's favourite leisure activities at Oxford were walking, horse-riding, boating and, of course, playing his beloved violin.

In Newman's *Idea of a University* he notes that the two orders of friars, the Dominican Blackfriars and Franciscan Greyfriars, developed half-detached from the university, insisting on their autonomy and providing for the instruction of their own students.

We students soon laid claim to the section of the library that suited us best. I was lucky enough to have a desk in a niche surrounded on three sides by Cardinal Newman's books. The pleasant musky smell from the old wooden book shelves and floor boards of this ancient Dominican friary lent an atmosphere of peaceful tranquillity to the surroundings, which would have matched the atmosphere of Trinity and Oriel where Newman had studied and taught.

When weather permitted, I gathered up my books and headed for a quiet spot under a tree or by the riverbank that borders Christchurch meadow, where the families of ducks and other wildlife seemed happy to share their space with this intruder, and I was very happy to enjoy their company.

One of my most memorable experiences of Oxford was of music—a subtle backdrop at Blackfriars as the friars practised for evening Mass, but also cascading from the various chapels and colleges as one moved about the city, particularly on Sundays and in the evenings during Evensong. Newman would have loved this aspect of Oxford, where, so often, he was to be found in the college chapel or happily playing his beloved violin in his rooms or at festive occasions.

Newman writes on the inspiration he found in music:

> I never wrote more than when I played the fiddle. I always sleep better after music. There must be some electric current passing from the strings through the fingers into the brain and down the spinal marrow. Perhaps thought is music.[2]

The 'Prayer Oratories' established by St Philip Neri, founder of the Oratorians, which involved gathering people around him for prayer and religious instruction, always included sacred music; 'some sacred music would be sung to refresh the spirits'. This would have been very important for Newman.

Notes

1.   Journal, March 1819: Newman, *Autobiographical Writings*.
2.   Newman, *Letters and Diaries*, vol. 22, p. 9, letter to R. W. Church, 11 July [1865].

5

The Annual Newman Pilgrimage to Littlemore

S HORTLY AFTER MY ARRIVAL IN OXFORD I was delighted
to join the first feast-day celebration of Blessed John
Henry Cardinal Newman, on 9 October 2010, with
a walk from the Oratory Church in Oxford to Littlemore
College. This 'night walk', attended by Newman's friends,
students and devotees, had been taking place for many
years, in hopeful anticipation of his canonization. So this
was a very special occasion.

FIRST STATION: THE OXFORD ORATORY

The Oratory Church of St Aloysius Gonzaga was the first
station of the walk. This church had been built by the Society
of Jesus in 1875 after the failure of Newman's attempts to
found an Oratory at Oxford.

In August 1864, Newman was offered a five-acre plot of
ground in Oxford, which its benefactor had hoped would
be used for a Catholic college. Newman knew he would find
it very difficult to face going back to Oxford, but he set his
heart on the idea of founding an Oxford Oratory to include
'a Centre and School of Catholicism in the heart of the University', something which would 'last and ... grow'.[1].

Bishop Ullathorne was in favour of the idea at first, but
Cardinal Manning, then Archbishop of Westminster, was

determined that young men should not go to Oxford, fearing they would lose their faith there, and he was equally determined that Newman should not go, fully aware that if he did Newman would draw young students there like 'flies round a honeypot'.[2] So sadly Newman was stopped from founding an Oxford oratory at that time. 'I see clearly that the real root of the difficulty is myself. There are those who cannot endure the thought that I should have the forming of the young Catholic mind at Oxford. This is the one point of battle.'[3] But a hundred years after his death, Newman's dream was fulfilled and the Oxford Oratory came into being, and this new saint is, indeed, drawing students here, with many of them taking instruction and entering the Catholic Church, as I personally witnessed.

Cardinal Newman did pay a return visit to Oxford on Trinity Sunday 1880 and preached at St Aloysius on that occasion. And so his voice was heard again from an Oxford pulpit, after a silence of a generation.

The Tyranny of Relativism

The Provost of the Oratory, speaking on this first feast day of Blessed John Henry Newman, referred to Newman's prophetic vision, in that he saw the rise of the 'relativism' so predominant in today's society. This, he explained, is the prevailing tide in society; that sees no objective truth in anything, that all views are of equal validity and that moral norms are nothing more than expediency. In a sermon preached in Birmingham in 1873 entitled 'The Infidelity of the Future', Cardinal Newman expressed his concern for what he termed this 'plague':

> The special peril of the time before us is the spread of that plague of infidelity . . . the elementary proposition of this new philosophy which is now so threatening us is this—that in all things we must go by reason, in nothing by faith, that things are known and are to be received so far as they can be proved.

Hence we have our modern obsession with science being the only arbiter of truth, said the Provost, adding that Newman 'went on to say that Catholics should expect to be slandered and persecuted by the modern means of communication because of their fidelity to faith'.

SECOND STATION: TRINITY COLLEGE

Here we reflected on the sixteen-year-old Newman arriving to take up the place he had been offered here at Trinity College on 8 June 1817 and on how he soon fell in love with Oxford. Newman opted for the pulpit after studying law for a short period. He was a very diligent and serious student, and this sensitive youth found certain aspects of college life a little boisterous. But Newman loved the college chapel, where he would often be found in prayer and reflection.

> I look at that communion table, and recollect with what feelings I went up to it in November 1817 for my first communion—how I was in mourning for the Princess Charlotte, and had black silk gloves—and the glove would not come off when I had to receive the Bread, and I had to tear it off and spoil it in my flurry.[4]

But this brilliant scholar only got a 3rd in his BA examination because he had been overly anxious, had studied too hard and read too widely without direction. Also, he was called to sit the examination a day sooner than expected, which may also have unnerved him a little.

Letter to his father, 1 December 1820

> It is all over, and I have not succeeded. The pain it gives me to be obliged to inform you and my mother of it, I cannot express.
> What I feel on my own account is indeed nothing at all, compared with the thought that I have disappointed you. And most willingly would I consent to a hundred

times the sadness that now overshadows me, if so doing would save my mother and you from feeling vexation. I will not attempt to describe what I have gone through, but it is passed away, and I feel quite lightened of a load. The examining masters were as kind as it was possible to be; but my nerves quite forsook me and I failed. I have done everything I could to attain my object; I have spared no labour, and my reputation in my college is as solid as before, if not so splendid. If a man falls in battle after a display of bravery, he is honoured as a hero; ought not the same glory to attend him who falls in the field of literary conflict?

THIRD STATION: ORIEL COLLEGE

Mr Newman is elected Fellow of Oriel. 'One of the happiest days of my life'. Despite his poor examination results, Newman was encouraged to try for an Oriel fellowship. He put his head down and studied for six months, and was delighted to be successful in the examinations at Easter 1822. At that time Oriel was regarded as intellectually the most outstanding college in Oxford University.

> On the Friday morning of Easter week as he sat playing the violin in his lodgings on Broad Street he heard a knock on his door. It was the Oriel butler. The butler, after recovering from a slight surprise at finding so scholarly a gentleman playing the fiddle at such an hour, made the usual formal speech. 'I have, sir, I fear, disagreeable news to announce. Mr Newman is elected Fellow of Oriel and his immediate presence is required there.' He went on fiddling. No sooner was the butler out of sight than the new Fellow 'was off long-leggedly down the High Street for Magpie Lane, at so extraordinary a pace ... that the tradesmen along the way rightly interpreted the bells ringing out from three towers to announce the election of a new Fellow ... [and] bowed in admiration at his success.[5]

As this was such a huge event in Newman's life, I had previously taken the time to trace his steps on that momentous day. So off I set, down Broad Street, on to the High Street and down Magpie Lane, joining the masses of students on the way—as would have been the case in Newman's time. I was imagining those bells ringing from the three towers and the admiration of the tradesmen, lifting their caps and perhaps even scratching their heads in disbelief at the sight of this scrawny young man, now a Fellow of Oriel.

> I pass on to Friday morning and my surprise on finding myself elected. I had to hasten to the round tower where we had been examined, to receive the congratulations of all the Fellows—I bore it till Keble took my hand, and then felt so abashed and unworthy the honour done me that I seemed desirous of quite sinking into the ground. I have since that time regularly for two days dined in the common room, and am abashed to find I must call them 'Hawkins', 'Keble','Tyler', etc.[6]

Newman seemed quite overwhelmed with his position at Oriel at first. Extremely shy, the studious youth kept mostly to himself, going for solitary walks and communicating very little with his peers. This changed with the help of a number of the more senior members of the college, who set about helping to get him out of his shell. It is noted that when Newman did start to speak, 'there was no stopping him'!

It was at Oriel that he met many of his eminent associates and good friends, amongst them John Keble, Edward Pusey and Hurrell Froude. Newman soon blossomed in the atmosphere of Oriel. In a letter to his brother Charles at the time he writes, 'I think myself honoured inexpressibly by being among such kind, liberal, candid, moderate, learned and pious men, as every act shows the fellows of Oriel as a body to be'.[7]

His father's death, 1824

'The dread event has happened. Is it possible? O my father, where art thou? I got to town Sunday morning. He knew me—tried to put out his hand and said "God bless you!"

Towards the evening of Monday he said his last words. He seemed in great peace of mind.'[8]

> *Farewell, but not forever! Brother dear,*
> *Be brave and patient on thy bed of sorrow;*
> *Swiftly shall pass thy night of trial here,*
> *And I will come and wake thee on the morrow.*
> From *The Dream of Gerontius*

John Henry had been helping his parents with the family finances for years, also with Aunt Betsey's debts, and with Frank's accommodation before he went to Oxford and often getting Charles 'out of a scrape'. He also helped with his sisters' education. But now he was determined to do even more to help his mother who had some money of her own, but often needed more.

FOURTH STATION: ST CLEMENTS

Ordained an Anglican priest in May 1825, Newman wrote, 'I have the responsibility of souls on me to the day of my death'.[9]

We stop to look at where the ancient church of St Clements once stood in the centre of the road, which became the open space called 'The Plain' when the church was demolished in 1829. It is now a roundabout. Here we remember that this was once sacred ground, where Newman served as curate following his ordination in the Church of England from 1824 to 1826.

During his time here he worked with extraordinary diligence, visiting the entire population of this small and then impoverished parish—including the Catholic priest—preaching and giving special attention to the sick and the elderly poor. He also helped raise the money for the new St Clement's church that replaced the ancient one. In a letter he explains that he also included the dissenters of the parish, telling them, 'I make no difference between you and church-goers—I count you all my flock, and shall be most happy to do you a service out of church, if I cannot within it'.[10]

Later that year Whately appointed Newman vice-principal of Alban Hall, a hall of residence for undergraduates. In 1826 he was made an official tutor of Oriel and next year he was appointed a public examiner.

Newman was extremely meticulous in helping his students, both as their teacher and lecturer, but he also became their friend, confidant and spiritual advisor. He was greatly liked and respected by them. It was not surprising that at this stage he felt he was becoming a little superior in his attitude, as he writes, 'The truth is I was beginning to prefer intellectual excellence to moral; I was drifting in the direction of the Liberalism of the day. I was rudely awakened from my dream at the end of 1827 by two great blows—illness and bereavement'.[11]

The first of these blows was soon to hit home as the overwork took its toll and he fell ill as a result of sheer exhaustion. The doctor told him he could not go on with his Oxford work and needed a break, so he took a week off to stay with friends and then went to his family, who had rented a house at Brighton.

His sister Mary's death—'Consolations in Bereavement'

Newman had many trials and sufferings during his early years at Oxford. It would seem that every time he was called home it was because of some new crisis in the family's financial affairs. But the heaviest blow of all and one that would weigh heavily on his shoulders for the rest of his life, took place on 4 January 1827, when he was home visiting the family. That evening his beloved sister Mary complained of not feeling well at the dinner table and asked to be excused to lie down. The doctor was called and, sadly, Mary died some hours later.

A devastated Newman writes:

> And how can I summon strength to recount the particulars of the heaviest affliction with which the good hand of God has ever visited me? For some time I had a presentiment more or less strong that we should lose

dear Mary. I was led to this by her extreme loveliness of character, and by the circumstance of my great affection for her. I thought I loved her too well, and hardly ever dared to take my full swing of enjoyment in her dear society. It must have been in October 1826 that, as I looked at her, beautiful as she was, I seemed to say to myself, not so much 'will you live?' as 'how strange that you are still alive![12]

Consolations in Bereavement

Death was full urgent with thee, sister dear,
And startling in his speed;
Brief pain, then languor till thy end came near;
Such was the path decreed,
The hurried road
To lead thy soul from earth to thine own God's abode.

Death wrought with thee, sweet maid, impatiently;
Yet merciful the haste
That baffles sickness;—dearest, thou didst die,
Thou wastn't made to taste
Death's bitterness,
Decline's slow-wasting charm, or fever's fierce distress.

Death came and went; that so thy image might
Our yearning hearts possess,
Associate with all pleasant thoughts, and bright
With youth and loveliness.
Sorrow can claim
Mary, nor lot, nor part in thy soft soothing name.

Joy of sad hearts, and light of downcast eyes!
Dearest thou art enshrined
In all thy fragrance in our memories;
For we must ever find
Bare thought of thee
Freshen this weary life, while weary life shall be.

Oxford, 1828

This beautifully sensitive poem must surely offer huge consolation to anyone who has suffered the loss of a young sibling.

After Mary's death, Newman had to go back to Oxford and get on with his life there, but it is said that throughout his life he never got over the death of this beloved sister.

FIFTH STATION:
THE UNIVERSITY CHURCH OF ST MARY THE VIRGIN

At this beautiful University Church we pay particular attention to the extraordinary south 'Virgin porch', designed by Nicholas Stone in 1637 and partly paid for by Archbishop Laud's chaplain, Dr Morgan Owen. In early Baroque style, it is highly ornate, with barley sugar-twist spiral columns supporting a curly broken pediment framing a shell niche with a statue of the Virgin and Child flanked by cherubs, underneath a Gothic fan vault. This is thought to be the first post-Reformation statue of the Blessed Virgin to have been erected in a prominent position in a public street in England, and is remarkable in having survived until Newman's time.

> I had a true devotion to the Blessed Virgin, in whose college I lived, whose altar I served, and whose Immaculate Purity I had in one of my earliest printed sermons made much of.[13]

From March 1828 to September 1843 Newman was vicar of this beautiful Gothic University Church of St Mary the Virgin, which stands on the main street in Oxford. This was where their dedicated pastor, in addition to his studies and preaching, worked tirelessly, helping countless people, both Catholic and non-Catholic, with their religious difficulties.

But it is for his prolific preaching that Newman is mostly remembered. Here I particularly wanted to see the pulpit where Newman preached such thought-provoking sermons, hoping against hope that it would still be in place. Thankfully, Oxford reveres its beautiful antiquity and so there it stood, this precious artefact, just as Newman had left it.

It was a cold dark night and the church was freezing, but this somehow provided a better sense of what it would have been like in Newman's time, lit by flickering gaslight, so I could more fully appreciate the atmosphere in which he held his audience enthralled.

Many people have written about Newman's preaching and the effect it had on his audience at St Mary's. Matthew Arnold's account is particularly beautiful: 'The charm of that spiritual apparition, gliding in the dim afternoon light through the aisles of St Mary's, rising into the pulpit, and then, in the most entrancing of voices, breaking the silence with words and thoughts which were a religious music, — "subtle, sweet, mournful"'.[14]

Newman and his friend Hurrell Froude believed that their duties towards their students as tutors should include more than their academic welfare. They felt they should also be guiding them spiritually. This got Newman into trouble with Hawkins the Provost, who didn't agree, and refused to allocate any more students to him at Oriel. It was recognized that he was having enormous influence on the undergraduates with his sermons, which would not have suited Hawkins. So storm clouds were gathering, and Newman had to resign his tutorship in 1830.

When Newman and his friends at Oriel were beginning their commitment to the renewal of the Anglican Church, Newman gave lectures here on Wednesday nights and began the practice of daily public prayer and weekly communion.

Newman the Preacher

Newman soon became the most popular and prolific preacher in Oxford. His preaching became one of the great attractions of the university. It is recorded that his church was packed to overflowing every Sunday as people from all sectors of society crammed to hear this gifted preacher. 'He laid his finger—how gently yet how powerfully—on some inner place in the hearer's heart and told him things about himself he had never known till then' (Principal Shairp).[15]

It is recorded that there were many occasions when Newman induced his audience to tears. A description of the
following dramatic scene is recorded and remembered: 'The
great church, the congregation all breathless with expectant
attention; the gaslight just at the left hand of the pulpit,
lowered that the preacher might not be dazzled.' The nine-
teen-year-old Henry William Wilberforce, who recorded
this, remembers standing in the half darkness, under the
gallery, as the drama unfolded, and still has in his ears the
sound of Newman's words:

> He never moved anything but his head. His hands never
> seen. His sermon began in a calm musical voice, his tone
> rising slightly as he went on; it seemed as if 'his soul
> and his body glowed with suppressed emotion'... at
> times pausing before adding a few weighty words. The
> very tones of his voice seemed as if they were something
> more than his own.[16]

'His soul was in his voice, as a bird is in its song,' wrote
Henry Scott Holland, while Matthew Arnold claims Newman had 'the most entrancing of voices, breaking the silence
with words and thoughts which were a religious music—
subtle, sweet, mournful', while Emily Bowles confesses that
she wept when she first heard this 'exquisite' voice ring out
from the pulpit.

One of Pope John XXIII's favourite maxims, 'The best
way to preach with success is to have a great love for Jesus
Christ', could certainly be said to apply to Cardinal Newman. 'He seemed to be addressing the most sacred con-
sciousness of each of us—as the eyes of a portrait appear
to look at every person in the room', as J. A. Froude noted.[17]

SIXTH STATION:
THE SITE OF THE ANGEL COACHING INN

A short distance from the beautiful collegiate church, on
the opposite side of the road, we come upon the site of the

former 'Angel', one of Oxford's famous coaching inns. This building, which is part of a hotel today, had been a centre for secret Masses during the persecutions of the sixteenth and seventeenth centuries. I wondered if they still have the 'priest's hole' here.

A testimony to the Catholic faith of the Oxford area is the considerable number of stately homes in and about the nearby countryside, such as Holywell and Stoner Manor, which contain the priest's holes that were used to shelter priests during Reformation times. These staunchly loyal Catholic families—the Napiers of Holywell and the Stoners of Stoner—if caught shielding a priest could have lost their homes and even their lives.

The most prominent saint martyr who was betrayed by priest hunters in the area was the Jesuit, St Edmund Campion, a former brilliant student of Oxford University, who was hung, drawn and quartered for the faith just a year after being ordained in Rome.

Blessed Dominic comes to Oxford

The date was Wednesday, 8 October 1845, a day of pouring rain. Fr Dominic Barberi was expected in the evening and Newman sent Dalgairns and St John to meet the coach at the Angel.

> Dalgairns writes: About 3 o'clock I went to take my hat and stick and walk across the fields to the Oxford 'Angel' where the coach stopped. As I was taking my stick Newman said to me in a very low and quiet tone, 'When you see your friend, will you tell him that I wish him to receive me into the Church of Christ?' I said 'Yes' and no more. I told Father Dominic as he was dismounting from the top of the coach. He said 'God be praised', and neither of us spoke again till we reached Littlemore.[18]

Blessed Dominic writes his own account of the evening:

> I left Aston on the 8th and reached Oxford at ten o'clock that night, soaked with rain. Hardly had I reached the

inn, when I found Mr Dalgairns waiting to take me to Littlemore, the monastery established about three years back by Rev. John Henry Newman. There these Oxford men lead a penitential life much more severe than that usually led by Religious.[19]

SEVENTH STATION:
THE CHURCH OF ST EDMUND AND ST FRIDESWIDE

Our next station is the church of St Edmund and St Frideswide, the home of the Franciscan friars, who served the surrounding parish and both study and teach in the University. They arrived in Oxford first in 1224, within the lifetime of St Francis, and although in Newman's time they were still in their long exile, he lamented their loss. He would have been glad to see their return, for he knew how important a contribution to the development of Christian doctrine was made by their great lecturer, Blessed Duns Scotus, 'who fired France for Mary without spot', and by the other teaching friars whom Newman lists:

> Alas! For centuries past this city had lost its prime honour and boast, as a servant and soldier of the Truth. Once named the second school of the Church, second only to Paris, the foster-mother of St Edmund, St Richard, St Thomas Cantilupe, the theatre of great intellects, of Scotus, the subtle Doctor, of Hales the irrefragable, of Occam the special, of Bacon the admirable, of Middleton the solid, and of Bradwardine the profound, Oxford has now lapsed to the level of mere human loveliness ... There are those who, having felt the influence of this ancient school, and being smit with its splendour and its sweetness, ask wistfully, if never again it is to be Catholic, or whether at least some footing for catholicity may not be found there. All honour and merit to the charitable and zealous hearts who so inquire![20]

EIGHTH STATION:
THE HOUSE WHERE MRS NEWMAN, HARRIETT AND
JEMIMA LIVED FROM 1833 TO 1836

Next we arrived at the house in Littlemore (now called Grove House) where Newman's mother and sisters, Harriett and Jemima, lived from 1833 until Mrs Newman's death in May 1836 and the sisters married two brothers. The Newman ladies were closely involved in helping Newman run his school and with various charitable works in the parish of Littlemore. Mrs Newman laid the foundation stone for the church that Newman built for his parishioners here and is commemorated in a plaque inside the church. But Newman knew that his mother did not share, and did not understand, his developing religious opinions:

> Nearly in the last conversation I had with her, I saw she quite mistook something I said and that she was hurt at it ... All this brought me to see that I had taken a false step in wishing her to be at Oxford. I can never repent it for the good she has done to Littlemore, and for your most happy marriage, but I myself suffered by it ... I know in my own heart how much I ever loved her, and know too how much she loved me—and often when I had no means of showing it, I was quite overpowered from the feeling of her kindness.[21]

NINTH STATION: THE COTTAGES

The next stop on our journey was before a pair of cottages in Rose Hill, Littlemore, that had been rented by the Newman family from 1830 to 1833: Mrs Newman and the girls lived in one, and the other was for John Henry as a retreat and study. During the cholera epidemic of 1831 these cottages became the headquarters for nurses and a depot for medicine, as John Henry and all his family worked tirelessly among the poor of Littlemore. His sister Harriett describes the family home here, and Newman's work on the Arians of the fourth century, and his greatest hero, St Athanasius:

> We are now quite settled ... The long vac. has begun
> and John has taken possession of his new apartments—
> consisting of a hall, staircase, study and bedroom—quite
> grand is he not? His study is very pretty and comfortable
> for summer. We have made a new large window in it,
> allowing him a view of our garden, and a very pleasant
> look out towards Oxford. He is very much charmed
> with all his arrangements, which we did not allow him
> to see till everything was completed.

TENTH STATION: THE SCHOOL AND A CHURCH THAT NEWMAN BUILT AT LITTLEMORE FOR HIS PARISHIONERS

The two historic buildings before which we stand—a little twin-gabled school and a simple early English chapel—were provided by Newman for his dear people of Littlemore, to 'feed them in both mind and soul'. His happiest moments were spent here among the children of the parish, but here also was the scene of that last Anglican sermon, a sad farewell, after so many hundreds of sermons, both parochial and plain. As Principal Shairp wrote,

> How vividly comes back the remembrance of the aching
> blank, the awful pause, which fell on Oxford when that
> voice had ceased, and we knew that we should hear it
> no more. It was as when, to one kneeling by night, in
> the silence of some vast cathedral, the great bell tolling
> solemnly overhead has suddenly gone still.[22]

Suffering and struggles on deciding to enter the Catholic Church

One can only marvel at the long interior struggle, the sacrifices and difficulties that this renowned scholar and Anglican clergyman had to endure because of his decision to enter the Roman Catholic Church. We get just a tiny indication of this in a letter he wrote to his beloved sister Jemima at the time: 'It pains me very deeply to pain you, but you see how I am forced to it. You will not say, I think, that I am less affectionate to you from the bottom of my heart and loving, than I ever have been.'[23]

His sister Harriett broke off all contact with him. His farewell to his devout Anglican friends, who didn't quite understand, was very painful. But the wrench from his beloved Oxford was huge.

Newman had previously thought that he would spend the remainder of his life at Oxford, which he dearly loved and where he had spent so many happy years, but this was not to be the case now. So the sacrifices he was making to enter what he termed 'the one fold of Christ' were enormous. But, certainly very upset at the behaviour of family members and friends, he was yet consumed with the joy of having become a Catholic—a joy that never left him.

He wrote to a 'very intimate friend' on 3 April 1843, when resigning as vicar of St Mary's:

> Accept this apology, my dear Church, and forgive me. As I say so, tears come into my eyes;—that arises from the accident of this time, when I am giving up so much I love ... How could I remain at St Mary's a hypocrite? ... That sort of dull aching pain is mine; but my responsibility really is nothing to what it would be, to be answerable for souls, for confiding loving souls, in the English Church, with my convictions.[24]

'The Parting of Friends' — Newman's famous farewell sermon

When Newman ultimately decided to enter the Catholic Church, in an emotional farewell to his beloved parishioners he preached his last sermon as an Anglican vicar at Littlemore on 25 September 1843. It is recorded that there was scarcely a dry eye in the congregation.

> And, O my brethren, O kind and affectionate hearts, O loving friends, should you know anyone whose lot

it has been, by writing or by word of mouth, in some degree to help you thus to act; if he has ever told you what you knew about yourselves, or what you did not know; has read to you your wants or feelings, and comforted you by the very reading; has made you feel that there was a higher life than this daily one, and a brighter world than that you see; or encouraged you, or sobered you, or opened a way to the enquiring, or soothed the perplexed; if what he has said or done has ever made you take interest in him, and feel well inclined towards him; remember such a one in time to come, though you hear him not, and pray for him, that in all things he may know God's will, and at all times he may be ready to fulfil it.[25]

In a letter to Richard Westmacott, Newman outlines his reasons for joining the Catholic Church:

I think the Church of Rome is in every respect the continuation of the early Church. I think she is the early Church in these times, and the early church is she in these times. They differ in doctrine and discipline as child and grown man differ, not otherwise. I do not see any medium between disowning Christianity, and taking the Church of Rome.[26]

Newman suffered much from the misunderstandings, suspicions and opposition of some ecclesiastical authorities at the time. This is why he later wrote his *Apologia*, to provide an explanation of his decision to enter the Catholic Church.

ELEVENTH STATION:
THE CHURCH OF BLESSED DOMINIC BARBERI

I am this night expecting Father Dominic the Passionist who from his youth has been led to distinct and direct thoughts, first of the countries of the North, then of England. After thirty years (almost) waiting, he was without his own act sent here. But he has had little to do with conversions. I saw him here for a few minutes on St John Baptist's Day last year. He is a simple, holy man, and withal gifted and remarkable powers. He does not know of my intention, but I mean to ask of him admission into *the One Fold of Christ*.[27]

TWELFTH STATION: LITTLEMORE COLLEGE

At last, at the end of our three-mile pilgrim journey, we had arrived at the building known as 'The College', at Littlemore. It was here on 8 October 1845 that John Henry Newman, Master of Arts and Bachelor of Divinity in the University of Oxford, once a priest of the Church of England, knelt in humble confession before the simple Italian preacher and asked to be permitted to enter 'the one fold of Christ'.

Blessed Dominic relates

As previously mentioned, Blessed Dominic arrived in Oxford soaked to the skin on that historic night; here he gives his own account of what happened:

> I arrived in Oxford, sodden with rain, a few hours before midnight. I went to Littlemore and whilst I was drying myself before the fire I turned round and what was my surprise at seeing Mr Newman kneeling before me, begging me to hear his confession and receive him into the Catholic Church. There, just beside the fire, he began his confession. Next morning I went to Oxford and said Mass in a Catholic chapel which I found there.[28]

The College was an old granary attached to a number of cottages and a stable that Newman had renovated and converted as a parsonage house at first, but after he entered the Catholic Church, it had become a peaceful retreat of prayer, fasting and study for him and some friends who joined him to form a small community, living a 'semi-monastic-style' life, something like what we read of in the lives of the Fathers of the desert, of praying, fasting, study.

In his *Apologia* Newman says that entering the Catholic Church was 'like coming into port after a rough sea'. Newman never regretted his decision and the joy he experienced never left him.

Notes

1   Newman, *Letters and Diaries*, vol. 1, pp. 133–4.

2   J. Sugg, *Snapdragon in the Wall: The Story of John Henry Newman*, Leominster: Gracewing, 2002, p. 34.

3   Newman, *Autobiographical Writings*, p. 201.

4   W. Ward, *The Life of John Henry Cardinal Newman, Based on his Private Journals and Correspondence*, 2 vols, London: Longmans, Green & Co., 1912; also Newman, *Letters and Diaries*, vol. 1, p. 48, note to 30 November 1817.

5   Newman, *Apologia*.

6   Newman, *Letters and Diaries*, vol. 1, pp. 131, 134, 139.

7   R. van de Weyer and P. Saunders, *I Step, I Mount, The Vision of John Henry Newman*, London: Marshall Morgan and Scott, 1989, p. 15.

8   Sugg, *Snapdragon on the Wall*, p. 25.

9   Newman, *Autobiographical Writings*, p. 201.

10 van de Weyer and Saunders, *I Step, I Mount*, p. 17.

11 Newman, *Apologia*.

12 *Ibid.*, ch. 5, on his sister Mary's death.

13 Newman, *Apologia*.

14 O. F. Cummings, *John Henry Newman and his Age*, New York: Cascade Books, 2019, p. 157.

15 John Campbell Shairp, a Presbyterian, who studied at Balliol 1840–4 and was stirred by John Henry Newman's Oxford sermons. In 1868 he became Principal of United College, St Andrew's.

16 Excerpt from Henry William Wilberforce's letter of 22 Sept 1843 to Newman's sister Jemima; J. A. Froude, *Short Studies on Great Subjects*, vol. 4, London: Longmans, Green & Co., 1899, p. 186.

17 Froude, *Short Studies*, vol. 4, letter 3.

18 Ward, *The Life of John Henry Cardinal Newman*, chapter 3.

19 Sugg, *Snapdragon in the Wall*, p. 91.

20 Newman, *The Idea of a University*, pp. 28, 31.

21 Newman, *Letters and Diaries*, vol. 5, p. 313, writing to his sister Jemima, and referring to her marriage on 27 April 1836, shortly before his mother's death on 17 May. See also Ker, *John Henry Newman*, p. 131.

22 R. H. Ellison (ed.), *The Victorian Pulpit, Spoken and Written Sermons in Nineteenth Century Britain*, London: Associated University Presses, 1998, p. 90.
23 Newman, *Letters and Correspondence of John Henry Newman*, ed. A. Mozley, London: Longmans, Green & Co., 1890, excerpt from letter to his sister Jemima, 22 September 1843.
24 Newman, *Apologia*.
25 Newman, *Letters and Diaries*, vol. 5, p. 9; *Sermons bearing on Subjects of the Day*, p. 409.
26 Newman, letter to Richard Westmacott, 11 July 1845, on reasons for joining the Catholic Church; D. Armstrong, *The Quotable Newman: A Definitive Guide to his Central Thoughts and Ideas*, New York: Sophia Institute Press, 2012.
27 Newman, *Letters and Diaries*, vol. 11, p. 6. *Apologia*, ed. M. Ward, p. 158.
28 Edmund Thorpe, CP, *Dominic Barberi, C.P., An Apostle of England*, chapter 3. See also Newman, *Letters and Diaries*, vol. 5, p. 313.

✣ 6 ✣

The Oxford Movement

*Speak I must, for the times are very evil yet no one
speaks against them.*

Newman, speaking at the start
of the Oxford Movement

T HE YEAR WAS 1833 and Newman and his friends, Hurrell Froude, John Keble and others, were anxious to reform the Anglican Church and reconnect it to its Catholic roots, which for centuries had been neglected.

In July, John Keble, whom Newman greatly admired, set a challenge by preaching a sermon entitled 'National Apostasy'. Newman, who was on his Mediterranean travels with Hurrell Froude at the time, had apparently given his consent for Keble to preach at the Collegiate Church during his absence.

Keble's challenge had to be taken up and the response by Newman and his friends saw the beginning of what became known as the Oxford Movement. He writes at the time:

> I thought the Anglican Church was tyrannized over by a mere party, and I aimed at bringing into effect the promise contained in the motto to the Lyra: 'They shall know the difference now.' I only asked to be allowed to show them the difference.[1]

> *Sensitiveness*
> *Time was, I shrank from what was right*
> *From fear of what was wrong;*
> *I would not brave the sacred fight,*
> *Because the foe was strong.*

51

So, when my Saviour calls, I rise,
And calmly do my best;
Leaving to Him, with silent eyes
Of hope and fear, the rest.

I step, I mount where He has led –
Men count my haltings o'er
I know them yet, though self I dread,
I love His precept more.

January 1833, Malta.

The Church is certainly in a wretched state, but not a gloomy one to those who regard every symptom of dissolution as a ground of hope … I see a system behind the existing one, a system indeed which will take time and suffering to bring us to adopt, but still a firm foundation.[2]

The method of this group, who came to be called 'Tractarians', was to circulate 'Tracts for the Times', in the form of pamphlets, to the clergy and others, pointing out abuses in the established Church and suggesting remedies. These were circulated between September 1833 and 1841, during the time when Newman was the much-sought-after vicar and preacher of the University Church of St Mary the Virgin.

Of the fundamental principles of the Tractarians, the first was that of dogma, as Newman writes: 'My battle was with liberalism; by liberalism I mean the anti-dogmatic principle and its developments. This was the first point on which I was certain.'[3]

Newman mostly uses poetry in the Tracts to get his message across. Even though he quite vehemently denies being a poet, many of his writings support the view that he is, indeed, a master of poetic verse. His poem 'The Pillar of the Cloud', alias 'Lead, Kindly Light', is included in the *Oxford Book of English Mystical Verse*.

But Newman is not concerned with his own profile as a poet, but sees the beauty of its rhetoric and persuasion as a means of introducing a message that cannot be so convincingly relayed in any other way, as he writes:

Do not stirring times bring out poets? Do they not give opportunity for the rhetoric of poetry and the persuasion? And may we not at least produce the shadows of high things, if not the high things themselves?[4]

Gradually, many came to realize that the result of the type of reform the Tractarians were advocating, spiritually, liturgically and theologically, would be Roman Catholicism. But this also came as a surprise to Newman and his friends, who had only set out to reform the Anglican Church.

LETTER TO WILLIAM PALMER, A MEMBER OF THE OXFORD MOVEMENT:

I would advocate a less formal scheme: not that I am not eventually for an association, but not till the Bishop puts himself at our head in this or that diocese. I would merely exert myself in my own place, and with my own immediate friends, in declaring and teaching the half-forgotten truths of Church union and order to all within my influence ... we print and circulate tracts, our friends in other dioceses read them, approve, and partly disapprove ... We try to get a footing in our county newspapers; and recommend our friends elsewhere to do the same.[5]

Tract 90: all hell broke loose when Newman wrote this tract, holding that the basic historical documents of the Church of England did not contradict the teachings of Rome. It provoked a storm of reaction against the movement and against him personally. This discovery had come primarily from his reading of the Fathers of the Church when preparing his essay on the development of Christian doctrine.

Thus the early Church Fathers, whom Newman so richly revered, played a crucial role in his decision to enter the Catholic Church. He relates the powerful contribution the following words of Augustine had on him, which, as he says, 'absolutely pulverized the theology of the Via Media', and as such became a huge turning point in Newman's life. He famously writes:

> For a mere sentence, the words of St Augustine struck
> me with a power which I never had felt from any words
> before ... they were like the 'Tolle, lege, — Tolle, lege',
> of the child, which converted St Augustine himself.
> *Securus judicat orbis terrarum!* [The verdict of the world
> is conclusive]'[6]

By those great words of the ancient Father, interpreting
and summing up the long and varied course of ecclesiastical history, the theology of the Via Media was absolutely
pulverized.

Notes

[1]   Newman, *Apologia*.
[2]   Extracts from a letter to former pupil, Robert Wilson, 31 March 1832.
[3]   Newman, *Apologia*.
[4]   Newman, *Letters and Diaries*, vol. 3, p. 121; *Apologia*, p. 45.
[5]   Newman, *Letters and Diaries*, vol. 4, pp. 86 ff., 26 December 1842.
[6]   Newman, *Apologia*. The words are taken from Augustine's *Contra Parmenianum*, and now form the motto of the Newman Society.

✛ 7 ✛

Catalogue of the English Saints

EWMAN HAS LEFT A VERY SPECIAL LEGACY to the English Church in that, during his time at Littlemore, he composed a monthly catalogue of the English saints, followed by a chronological arrangement starting from the second century.[1]

> I have here an opportunity of preserving, what otherwise would be lost ... And there are special reasons at this time for recurring to the saints of our own dear and glorious, most favoured, yet most erring and most unfortunate England...to teach us to love our country better and on truer ground, than heretofore; to teach us to invest her territory, her cities and villages, her hills and springs, with sacred associations; to give us an insight into her present historical position in the course of the Divine Dispensation; to instruct us in the capabilities of the English character; and to open upon us the duties and the hopes to which that Church is heir, which was in former times the Mother of St Boniface and St Etheldreda.[2]

Notes

[1] Newman makes no distinction between 'English' and 'British'; the English were not, of course, in fact present in Britain in Roman times.

[2] Newman, *Apologia*.

☩ 8 ☩

Leaving Littlemore

A s NEWMAN CONCLUDES HIS HISTORY of himself in his *Apologia* we see, yet again, the pain he had gone through in parting with those friends at Oxford who were his 'daily solace and relief' and all his 'thorough' friends who showed him 'true attachment' in past times.

At first Newman thought he would remain at Littlemore, but then decided to leave with his friends. The difficulties he was experiencing from different sectors of the Oxford community as a result of his decision, as a high-profile figure of the Anglican Church, to enter the much-hated Catholic Church, made it nigh impossible for him to remain. 'I cannot walk into or out of my house but curious eyes are upon me.'[1]

On his forty-fifth birthday, 21 February 1846, Newman said good-bye to his beloved Littlemore. Broken-hearted, his writing allows us a glimpse of his sense of sadness:

> Another comfort amid the pain of quitting this place is the pleasant memory which attaches to it. In spite of my having been in such doubt and suspense, it has been the happiest time of my life, because so quiet. Perhaps, I shall never have such quiet again.

So he put his books in crates, 'kissed the mantelpiece and the bed', and left.[2]

His account of his leaving Littlemore in his *Apologia* has the semblance of an Irish wake, where an emigrant is leaving for America, never again to return to Ireland or to meet his family and friends, so he is waked as though he has died.

As Newman describes, 'various friends came to see the last
of me'. He was certainly broken-hearted. Yet, again we see
him reaching out to someone in need of his help:

> Do not then be cast down, if you, though not very aged,
> feel less fervent than you did ten years since –only let it
> be a call on you to seek, grace to supply nature, as well
> as to overcome it. Put yourself ever fully and utterly
> into Mary's hands, and she will nurse you and bring
> you forward. She will watch over you as a mother over
> a sick child.[3]

Notes

1   Sugg, *Snapdragon in the Wall*, p. 91.
2   Newman, *Letters and Diaries*, vol. 11, p. 132; also *Apologia*.
3   Newman, letter to George Ryder.

Littlemore in the Snow

N EWMAN'S HERO IN *Loss and Gain*—one of only two novels Newman wrote—climbed one night to the top of one of the Oxford Towers to make observations of the stars.[1]

I remembered this sketch on an exceptionally cold and frosty night that winter, when I cautiously picked my way along the icy footpaths of the quiet Oxford village of Littlemore. The countryside all around was covered in a blanket of snow, and trees and hedgerows, sculpted in frost, glistened in the darkness under a sky lit by a thousand stars. With carefully measured steps I moved along through a timeless, silent wonderland of peaceful tranquillity and indescribable beauty.

In such a setting it was easy to recall—as I had set out to do—those mid-nineteenth-century times when the beloved Mr Newman, vicar of St Mary the Virgin in Oxford, purposefully strode about this then-impoverished parish, conducting chapel services, visiting the sick, holding catechism classes, running the school he built for his parishioners and—with the help of his sisters—teaching the children catechism and music, even providing pinafores for the children to wear to school.

Note

[1] O'Faolain, *Newman's Way*, p. 70.

Maryvale

No one has access to the almighty as his mother has.
Newman, *Meditations and Devotions*

NEWMAN AND HIS FRIENDS FROM LITTLEMORE moved to a house given to them by Bishop Wiseman near his seminary at Oscott, Birmingham, which they named Maryvale. Newman named every church, chapel and religious establishment he had been connected with after the Blessed Virgin, to whom he always had a special devotion even as an Anglican. He believed that his years at Oxford had been under the protection of Our Lady and that he was guided by her throughout his search for the Catholic Church. 'I had a true devotion to the Blessed Virgin, in whose college I lived, whose altar I served, and whose Immaculate Purity I had in one of my earliest sermon made much of'.[1]

The following June, Newman, St John and some of their group at Maryvale received Minor Orders at Oscott. Afterwards Wiseman arranged for Newman and St John to go to Rome for studies at the Propaganda College.

They set off that autumn for Rome via Paris, where they visited the shrine of Notre Dame des Victoires in thanksgiving for prayers offered there for Newman by the Fraternity of the Immaculate Heart of Mary. Then they travelled on to Milan, where they spent five weeks.

Newman was totally captivated by the beauty of Milan's churches and the presence of the Blessed Sacrament, 'ever ready to welcome the worshipper'. The unity of the Church, ever close to his heart, is brought home to him here:

> Here are a score of churches which are open to the passer by ... and the Blessed Sacrament ready for the worshipper even before he enters. There is nothing which has brought home to me so much the unity of the Church as the presence of its Divine Founder and Life wherever I go—all places are, as it were, one.[2]

It is thought that it was at that time, overwhelmed by the beauty of Milan's *duomo*—'an overpowering place'—that Newman wrote his famous account of the beauty of a Catholic cathedral.[3]

Newman made four visits to Rome in his lifetime, which we will examine in detail shortly.

ADVICE ON THE ROSARY
TO THE BOYS OF THE ORATORY SCHOOL

Newman loved the Rosary, and obviously wanted to share this special devotion to the Blessed Virgin particularly with the young. We here relate how he presents an inspiring meditation on the Rosary to the boys of the Oratory school: 'My dear boys, it seems so simple and easy, but you know God chooses the small things of the world to humble the great', he begins.

He speaks of something familiar to them, their own family, and relates this to the family in which God dwelt with his Blessed Mother and St Joseph. Next, to prepare them for the difficulties they should expect to meet in life, he urges them to put their faith and their love of the Rosary to practical use:

> This is what I should most wish you to remember in future years. For you will all have to go out into the world and going out into the world means leaving home ... but most men who know the world find it a world of great trouble, and disappointments, and even misery.

Maryvale

If it turns out so to you seek a home in the Holy Family
that you think about in the mysteries of the Rosary.[4]

Notes

1 Newman, *Apologia*.
2 Newman, *Letters and Diaries*, vol. 11, pp. 249–54.
3 *Ibid.*, p. 253.
4 P. Boyce, *Mary: The Virgin Mary in the Life and Writings of John Henry Newman*, Leominster: Gracewing, 2001, p. 182.

✛ 11 ✛

'Speak I Must'

All it takes for evil to prosper
is for good men to remain silent.
Edmund Burke

SPEAKING OUT BOLDLY AND UNAPOLOGETICALLY often caused Newman a great deal of suffering, but despite this, his was a consistent voice, challenging, defending and offering support and encouragement when needed: 'that I may cheerfully resign myself to such trouble or anxiety as necessary befalls anyone who has spoken boldly on an unpopular subject in a difficult time, with the confidence that no trouble or anxiety but will bring some real good with it in the event'.[1]

Because of the national uproar that had ensued against Catholics after the announcement of the restoration of the Roman Catholic hierarchy of England and Wales in 1850, Newman feared an outbreak of violent attacks against the Catholic population. This fear was compounded when an article appeared in *The Times* on 14 October 1850, stating that the restoration of the hierarchy was 'one of the grossest acts of folly and impertinence which the Court of Rome has ventured to commit since the Crown and people of England threw off its yoke'.[2]

In 1850 Newman had delivered a series of lectures defending the restoration, published as *Certain Difficulties Felt by Anglicans in Catholic Teaching*.

He now decided that he had to act to try to subdue the situation, so despite many other demands on his time, such as the setting up of the Oratory in Birmingham and his work on behalf of the Dublin university, he set about preparing a series of lectures in defence of Catholicism, *Lectures on the Present Position of Catholics in England*, addressed to the brothers of the Oratory (a group of laymen attached to the Oratorians), which he delivered at the Birmingham Corn Exchange from June to September 1851. Newman arranged for the press to be invited to ensure the message reached the ears of the general public.

The following comment is certainly full of wisdom. It is a tactic commonly used in advertising and other areas today by people or groups insistent on pushing their own agenda through media channels and public demonstrations:

> a fact or argument is not stronger in its own nature by being repeated; but the effect on any mind, which is passive under the indiction, is stronger and stronger every time it is repeated. In this way almost any idea whatever may be impressed on the mind; a man will begin at length to think himself a fool or a knave, if everyone tells him so.[3]

In these lectures, whilst censuring the perpetrators, he advises his listeners to act with dignity towards them.

In this beautiful, heart-rending address, he appeals to the British sense of right-mindedness and national pride:

> Where are ... the tender hearts, the kind feelings, the upright understandings of our countrymen and countrywomen? Where is the generosity of the Briton, of which from one's youth up one has been so proud? Where is his love of fair play, and his compassion for the weak, and his indignation at the oppressor, when we (Catholics) are concerned.[4]

In these lectures Newman provides an insight into how a country that was so Catholic, and had such a devotion to the Blessed Virgin that it came to be called 'the Dowry of Mary', turned against the Catholic Church and the Pope, calling him 'the Antichrist' at the Reformation.

He explains that the multitude would never have been converted by exact reasoning and facts that could be proved; 'so its upholders were clever enough to call the Pope Antichrist, and they let the startling accusation sink into people's minds, as nothing else would have succeeded'. This accusation would suggest a form of brainwashing—this is something he pursues throughout; the punch line delivered by Newman is that 'they pursue the same tactics now'.[5]

> As to the Catholic religion in England at the present day, this only will I observe, that the truest expedience is to answer right out, when you are asked; that the wisest economy is to have no management; that the best prudence is not to be a coward; that the most damaging folly is to be found out shuffling; and that the first of virtues is to 'tell truth, and shame the devil'.[6]

We see Newman involved in many other disputes in defence of the Catholic Church. He argued about Catholic doctrine and devotion with his friend Edward Pusey in relation to devotion to the Blessed Virgin Mary and with William Gladstone about papal infallibility and the Vatican Council decrees. Yet he confesses:

> I confess I have no love of suffering at all; nor am I at a time in life when a man commonly loves to risk it. To be quiet and to be undisturbed, to be at peace with all, to live in the sight of my Brethren, to meditate on the future and to die, such is the prospect, which is rather suitable to such as me.[7]

Always the gentleman, Newman looked for a moderate way in dealing with controversy. He had argued as an Anglican that the Church of England was a middle way, a Via Media, between Protestant and Catholic claims. He later abandoned this position, but was keen to be true to the moderation that inspired it.

Notes

1   Newman, *Lectures on the Present Position of Catholics in England*, p. 403.

2   A. O. J. Cockshut, 'The Literary and Historical Significance of the "Present Position of Catholics"', in *Newman after a Hundred Years*, ed. I. Ker and A. G. Hill. Oxford: Clarendon Press, pp. 111–27, at p. 119.

3   Newman, *Lectures on the Present Position of Catholics in England*, p. 230.

4   *Ibid.*, p. 235.

5   *Ibid.*, p. 129.

6   Newman, *Apologia*.

7   *Ibid.*

✢ 12 ✢

Dublin,
Newman's Catholic University

'O UR UNIVERSITY is destined for great things,' wrote
Newman at the commencement of his enterprise
in Ireland.[1] Dr Donal McCartney, Professor Emeritus of Modern History at University College Dublin, writes
that 'It was that conviction which remained an inspiration
and sustained UCD through the most difficult periods of
its history'.[2]

Our next destination is Dublin, where in 1851 Newman
was invited to set up a Catholic University by the Irish primate, Archbishop Paul Cullen, and to become its founding
rector. 'From first to last, education, in the large sense of the
word, has been my line.'[3]

Ireland at the time was a country recovering from the
Great Famine and the Catholic Church was being re-established after centuries of suppression under the Penal Laws.
It was also only two decades since Catholic emancipation,
so the Irish primate had a huge job in hand building up
parochial and diocesan structures.

In 1850 the Pope asked the Irish bishops, gathered at the
national synod in Thurles, to establish a Catholic university
in Ireland in a bid to combat the secular Queen's colleges
then being set up by the British government in Ireland.
Rome was totally against these colleges, urging instead
that the Irish bishops set up their own Catholic university
on the model of the Belgian Louvain.[4]

To get the Catholic university under way a university committee was subsequently set up at Thurles, consisting of archbishops, bishops, clergy and laymen of substance nominated by the bishops, which included Charles Bianconi (the pioneer of road transport in Ireland), all headed by Archbishop Cullen.

In England also the diocesan episcopacy was being re-established for the first time since the Reformation and the first synod of the new English hierarchy was held at Oscott in 1852.

THE ROAD TO THE UNIVERSITY:
'FIRST GET NEWMAN'

The road to setting up Dublin's Catholic University was not easy. Initially in April 1851, Cullen asked Newman if he would be prepared to advise on the appointment of staff and if he could 'spare time' to give some lectures on education in preparation for the opening of the university.

Cullen had been advised that the prestige of the proposed university would be greatly enhanced by aiming to get as head 'the most famous of all English-speaking Catholics'.[5] And so, because of his renowned intellectual capabilities, his experience as a highly respected academic at Oxford University, coupled with the fact that he has become a convert to Catholicism and a Roman Catholic priest, Newman was seen as the ideal candidate for the mammoth task, if he could be prevailed upon to accept it.

Cullen paid two visits to Newman at the Birmingham Oratory in July, the first en route to London to a meeting with prominent English Catholics, including the future Cardinal Manning. On his return journey he went via Birmingham to try to persuade Newman to become the first rector of the proposed university.

The convert lawyer and Member of Parliament, James Robert Hope, had told Cullen that the prestige of the Catholic University would be enhanced by associating it with the most famous name of all among English-speaking Catholics. 'First get Newman.'[6]

The timing, however, was not good for Newman, who had numerous pressures to contend with, including the nasty Achilli affair and the Oratory in Birmingham which was under construction. Also at this time he was preparing those crucially important lectures in defence of Catholicism in England.

Newman was also concerned that the post of rector of the university might not be compatible with his Oratorian vocation and suggested that he should just be 'Prefect of Studies', to take 'a temporary office'. He told Cullen: 'What I should desire is to do as much work for the University as possible with as little absence as possible from this place [Birmingham]. This problem being satisfied, I do not care what you are pleased to make me.'[7]

'IT NEEDED NEWMAN'

His Oratorian brothers, however, advised him to accept the offer of rector, urging that for the success of the university 'it needed Newman'.[8]

We note that Newman was gradually becoming enthusiastic about the project, as he writes, 'It will be the Catholic University of the English tongue for the whole world'.[9]

Through his lived experience of university life from the age of sixteen at his beloved Oxford, Newman had had a long-held idea for an ideal Catholic university and saw this as the opportunity to make this ideal become a reality. So in September he wrote to Cullen, who had now become Archbishop of Dublin, to say that he would 'most readily' give the lectures. However, he admitted that he knew very little about Ireland. And Newman did like to know his audience; 'but I consider I ought to know better than I do the state of public opinion and knowledge in Ireland on the subject of education, and your own ideas what lectures ought to be about, in order to be useful'.[10]

On 1 October 1851 Newman made his first visit to Ireland. After a rough sea passage, he arrived in Thurles to meet with Dr Patrick Leahy and Myles O'Reilly. This trio formed a sub-committee for the university. They drafted a report, the result of which was the first clear picture of the proposed university. The report comprised elements from the Oxford system, from Louvain and Newman's own priorities.

Newman then travelled to Drogheda to discuss the draft with Cullen, and paid courtesy calls to Maynooth and All Hallows in Dublin before returning to Birmingham on 8 October—an itinerary made possible only by the railway system then being installed in Ireland.

Crucially Newman saw a further opportunity in accepting the position as head of Ireland's Catholic University, in that he would be renewing the 'battle' against liberalism that was raging in Oxford twenty years before. But, even though he would not have his friends of the Oxford Movement to support him in Dublin he believed he would have the support of the Catholic Church, as he writes:

> It is a most daring attempt but first it is a religious one, next it has the Pope's blessing on it. Curious it will be if Oxford is imported into Ireland, not in its members only, but in its principles, methods, ways and arguments. The battle there will be what it was in Oxford twenty years ago ... It is very wonderful—Keble, Pusey, Maurice, Sewell, etc., who have been able to do so little against Liberalism in Oxford, will be renewing the fight, alas, not in their persons, in Ireland.[11]

The university committee adopted the proposed report drafted by the sub-committee in Thurles and on 12 November 1851 John Henry Newman was officially appointed Rector of the Catholic University. It was agreed that he would have complete control under the bishops.

Newman set out for Dublin on 7 May 1852 to present his 'few lectures on education' as requested by Cullen. Initially finding lodgings for himself at 22 Lower Dorset Street in Dublin, he had decided not to stay with his friend, the convert clergyman, Henry Wilberforce, fearing it would give the impression that the university might be dominated by Englishmen. But Dorset Street was also convenient since he could celebrate Mass in St Francis Xavier's Jesuit church in nearby Gardiner Street.

Newman quickly came to realize the immensity of the work that had to be done. In a letter to Ambrose St John he mentioned the possibility of setting up a Dublin Oratory to justify his presence in Ireland.

The newly appointed rector soon moved to more permanent lodgings in Harcourt Street in Dublin. In further letters to Ambrose St John and his fellow Oratorians in Birmingham, he recounted some humorous incidents about his experiences with the various 'poor servant girls' and housekeepers he encountered:

> When I got here, I found that the housekeeper ... had arranged not only my clothes but all my papers for me ... She had mixed everything, laying them most neatly according to their size. To this moment I have not had the courage to attempt to set them right ... She has taken to fill my drawers—but here she is beyond her province, and I have been obliged to snub her just now. As I generally seem very cross or very stupid, sometimes both, she puts me down doubtless as a specimen of an English priest.[12]

Notes

1   Newman, *Historical Sketches*, vol. 3, p. 146.
2   D. McCartney, *UCD: A National Idea. The History of University College Dublin*, Dublin: Gill & Macmillan, 1999, pp. 2–3.
3   Newman, *Apologia*.
4   L. McRedmond, *Thrown among Strangers, John Henry Newman in Ireland*. Dublin: Veritas, 1990, p. 47.
5   *Ibid.*, p. 47.
6   Newman, *Letters and Diaries*, vol. 14, p. 316.

7   McRedmond, *Thrown among Strangers*, p. 49.
8   Newman, *Letters and Diaries*, vol. 14, p. 262 n. 2
9   *Ibid.*, pp. 357–8.
10   *Ibid.*, pp. 389–90.
11   *Ibid.*, pp. 389–90; Ker, *John Henry Newman*, pp. 377–8.
12   Newman, *Letters and Diaries*, vol. 15, p. 88.

✠ 13 ✠

The Discourses:
The Idea of a University

ANYONE WHO HAS BURNED the midnight oil preparing a lecture for presentation will sympathize with Newman's struggle in formulating his Dublin discourses, which, he later disclosed, had given him 'more trouble than ever anyone with a stretch of fancy can conceive'. In exasperation, he writes, 'I have written reams of paper—finished, set aside—then taken them up again, and plucked them'.[1] One of his difficulties in preparing these lectures was that he liked to know his audience, and in Dublin he was on unfamiliar territory. 'The truth is, I have the utmost difficulty of writing to people I do not know'.[2]

And he did have reason for concern. Firstly, he had to follow Dr Cullen's brief that the university would be Catholic. He also had to allay the concerns of the Irish nationalists, who would perhaps think that the university might not be properly Irish, so he sensed he shouldn't say too much about Oxford. Archbishop Murray's view about the impracticability of the university also had to be taken into account. Newman decided that his major emphases in this first discourse, entitled 'University Teaching', would be on the place of religion in education and the value of education in its own right. 'From first to last, education, in the large sense of the word, has been my line', Newman stated.

Thus, extraordinary tact and diplomacy was needed in spades. Rector Newman set about presenting his first discourse on 10 May 1852 in the Exhibition Room at the Rotunda, where public meetings in Dublin normally took place. Ever the gentleman, Newman adopted a courteous, even apologetic, approach, assuring his audience that he was aware that his knowledge of 'the state of things in Ireland' was limited:

> What do I know of the state of things in Ireland that I should presume to put ideas of mine that could not be right except by accident, by the side of theirs, who speak in the country of their birth and their home? Gentlemen, you are natural judges of the difficulties which beset us, and they are doubtless greater than I can ever forebode.[3]

UNITING OXFORD, DUBLIN AND ROME

His discourse that evening marked the beginning of Newman's passionate presentations on the subject of the advantages of a liberal or philosophical education: 'The subject of liberal education and the principles on which it must be conducted have ever had a hold upon my own mind.'[4]

Newman's liberal or philosophical education is about the pursuit of knowledge for its own sake. He establishes the principle that knowledge is its own reward, and when considered in this light, is called 'liberal knowledge', and is the scope of academic institutions.[5]

For Newman, theology, man's knowledge of God, is a major branch of universal knowledge, and, as such, needs to be taught at a university. So at his Catholic University in Ireland, the input of theology was essential:

> Religious truth is not only a portion, but a condition of general knowledge. To blot it out is nothing short ... of unravelling the web of university teaching. It is, according to the Greek proverb, to take the 'spring from out of the year'; it is to imitate the preposterous proceeding of those tragedians who represented a drama with the omission of its principal part.[6]

Newman stresses that the Church has never been biased in the broadness of its scope and has ever even used unbelievers and pagans in evidence to her truth, as far as their testimony went. 'She avails herself of scholars, critics, and antiquarians, who are not of her communion … St Cyprian called Tertullian his master; St Augustine refers to Ticonius.'[7]

He also acknowledges that at times, 'a system of what is called secular education, in which theology and the sciences are taught separately, may, in a particular place or time, be the least of evils'.

HISTORY OF CELTIC MONASTIC SCHOOLS

Newman may not have known much about the state of things in Ireland at the time, but he certainly knew a great deal about the rich history of education in Ireland in the early centuries of Christianity and about the famous monastic schools of the early Irish monks, that brought the 'faith and the civilization' to Europe.[8]

We see Newman, the brilliant strategist, engaging with his audience about their heritage, of which he emphasizes they can justifiably be proud. An important factor he relates is that the proposed Catholic university has the support of the Bishop of Rome, who once gave both England and Ireland the faith and the civilization that united them in that 'memorable time'.[9] 'When the Celt and the Saxon were like savages, it was the See of Peter that gave both of them, first faith, then civilization; and then again bound them together in one by the seal of a joint commission to convert and illuminate, in their turn, the pagan continent.'[10]

He recounts that Ireland became the 'very wonder and asylum of all people by reason of its knowledge, sacred and profane, and the asylum of religion, literature and science' for those who were 'chased away from the continent by the barbarian invaders'.[11]

It was in those glory days of Celtic monasticism 'when St Aidan and the Irish monks went to Lindisfarne and Melrose and taught the Saxon youth; and when a St Cuthbert and a St Eata repaid their charitable toil; and when the English went to Ireland "numerous as bees", and the Saxon St Egbert and St Willibrord made the voyage to Ireland to prepare themselves for their work with the "heathen Frisians".'[12]

It was Alcuin, the pupil both of the English and Irish Schools—representative both of the Saxon and the Celt—who was the chief of those responsible for the foundation of the famous school of Paris set up by Charlemagne. 'When Charlemagne would revive science and letters in his own France, it was Alcuin, the representative of both the Saxon and the Celt, who was chief of those who went forth to supply the need of the great Emperor'.[13] Thus 'the two islands, England and Ireland, in a dark and dreary age, were the two lights of Christendom'.[14]

Newman's appeal to his audience that evening was that they now had a new mission and a new challenge assigned to them by the Pope in the setting up of Dublin's Catholic University:

> England and Ireland are not what they once were, but Rome is where it was, and St Peter is the same ... He of old made the two islands one by giving them joint work of teaching; and now surely he is giving us a like mission, and we shall become one again (in faith) while we zealously and lovingly fulfil it.[15]

His strongest point is that the appeal for the Catholic University comes from the Pope: 'It is the decision of the Holy See: St Peter has spoken ... He has spoken and has a claim on us to trust him.'[16]

DISCOURSES WELL RECEIVED

It must have been a wonderful experience to be present at that historic meeting that paved the way for Ireland's first

Catholic university, which has grown to become University College Dublin—Ireland's largest university today. Newman's audience that evening were listening to somebody who was the personification of what he was preaching. Here before them was a renowned classical scholar who had given up his prestigious position as an Oxford academic and much, much more, to follow the truth he had found in the Catholic Church.

They would also have appreciated the fact that this high-profile English convert was prepared to give his time and his vast educational knowledge and proficiency to help set up a Catholic university in Ireland, a country and a people largely unknown to him. A friend, who could not understand why Newman had taken on such a mammoth task, put this question to him: 'But what on earth possessed you, my good friend, to have anything to do with the Irish university? What was it to you? What was Ireland to you? You had your line and your work; was not that enough?'[17]

Afterwards Newman was told that 'all the intellect, almost, of Dublin was there'. Leading members of the clergy and laity, who had previously supported the Queen's colleges, seemed to have become interested, if not entirely 'won over'. He noted that some ladies were also present and there was a certain shuffling in the room as he addressed the group as 'not ladies and gentlemen', but, falling into his accustomed mode for addressing audiences of male students at Oxford, as 'gentlemen'.

A delighted and relieved Newman wrote to his friend at the Birmingham Oratory, Ambrose St John, to say that 'thanks to Our Lady', it seemed to have been 'a hit'.[18]

It is a tribute to Newman's extraordinary gift as a communicator that he managed to succeed in gaining the confidence of such a diverse group.

The second lecture took place at the concert room at the Rotunda a week later. He was

> amused at the great cleverness of the Irish, which surpasses anything I ever saw elsewhere. The very

ticket takers in the room followed my arguments, and gave an analysis of the Discourse afterwards. The printer makes most judicious remarks and alterations in the proof—always clever and well meant, though generally wrong.[19]

FURTHER DISCOURSES

Newman delivered three more discourses over the following three Mondays. His rhetoric was never dry or tedious, as he presented his 'well-thought-out' ideas for his university:

He saw literature—'the personal use or exercise of language'—as 'a gift as great as any that can be named', and stressed that 'the Classics have ever on the whole been the instruments of education' which Western civilization has adopted. Poetically, he exclaims, 'the perfection of the intellect, which is the aim of such an ideal education', may have 'almost the beauty and harmony of heavenly contemplation, so intimate is it with the eternal order of things and the music of the spheres'.[20]

Newman accepts that a university with a 'heathen code of ethics' does indeed produce leaders in every sector of society:

> Such a university—as Oxford showed—with a 'heathen code of ethics', at least can boast of a succession of heroes and statesmen, of literary men and philosophers, of men conspicuous for great natural virtues, for habits of business, for knowledge of life, for practical judgment, for cultivated tastes, for accomplishments who have made England what it is.[21]

Newman's aim for his students was that they should mature not just as gentlemen, but as Christian gentlemen, and therefore theology should be taught: 'Theology is a real science: we cannot exclude it and still call ourselves philosophers. If the Catholic faith is true a university cannot exist externally to the Catholic pale, for it cannot teach Universal Knowledge if it does not teach Catholic theology'.[22]

Central to everything else is that 'truth is the object of knowledge of whatever kind' and it is the knowledge of this truth which the human mind seeks to contemplate. Newman's main point is that 'Behind the veil of the visible universe, there is an intelligent Being, acting on and through it, as and when He will'.[23]

Importantly, Newman believed that his presentations in the discourses could only be understood within a unified concept. You could not accept it in part and reject the rest. It would be important to read the whole rather than examine any one of the discourses in detail.

Notes

1   Newman, *Letters and Diaries*, vol. 15, pp. 66–7.
2   *Ibid.*; Ker, *John Henry Newman*, pp. 378–9.
3   Newman, *University Teaching Considered in Nine Discourses*, p. 12.
4   *Ibid.*, p. 1.
5   *Ibid.*, p. 174.
6   *Ibid.*, p. 68
7   *Ibid.*, p. 7.
8   *Ibid.*, p. 15.
9   *Ibid.*, p. 17.
10   *Ibid.*, p. 15.
11   *Ibid.*
12   *Ibid.*, pp. 16–17.
13   *Ibid.*, p. 17.
14   *Ibid.*, p. 16.
15   *Ibid.*, p. 17.
16   *Ibid.*, p. 13.
17   T. Iglesias, 'Why did Newman come to Dublin?', *The Irish Catholic*, 10 October 2019 (Prof. Emerita Teresa Iglesias is the founding director of the International Centre for Newman Studies at University College Dublin).
18   Newman, *Letters and Diaries*, vol. 15, pp. 83–4; Ker, *John Henry Newman*, p. 379.
19   Newman, *Letters and Diaries*, vol. 15, p. 88.
20   Newman, *The Idea of a University*.
21   *Ibid.*

22   *Ibid.*
23   *Ibid.*

✠ 14 ✠

Public Lecture
at University College Dublin

HE TERM 'LIBERAL' in general today assumes something without boundaries or limits, which is why
Newman's vision of liberal education is often misunderstood in the context of modern assumptions about
education. The Newman scholar, Professor Ian Ker, stressed
at a public lecture discussing the challenges faced by Newman in coming to Ireland to establish the Catholic University (held on 9 October 2019 at University College Dublin,
prior to Cardinal Newman's canonization in October 2019),
that what Newman meant by 'liberal education' has been
much misunderstood: 'When Newman speaks about liberal
education, he isn't speaking about the liberal arts ... it is any
subject that could encourage the student to think', adding
that 'He didn't approve of subjects where you simply had
to remember a lot of stuff'. Dr Ker explained that Newman
was very clear that a proper education would allow students
to make judgements. He reminds listeners that Newman,
whom we view chiefly as a theologian, said, 'From first
to last, education, in the large sense of the word, has been
my line'.

Dr Donal McCartney is keen to clarify that Newman's
university was not restricted to or hampered by a classical
education:

> Newman strove for a proper balance between utilitarian
> and liberal objectives. He not only sought to preserve

what was best in the older university courses but was also eager to have his university respond to the needs and the developments and ever widening field of knowledge of his own time. He knew the value of an education in the classics; but any notions that his university was therefore hampered by, or restricted to, a classical education are very wide of the mark.[1]

Note

[1]   McCartney, *University College Dublin*.

✠ 15 ✠

To Tervoe for a Rest and Silence

N	EWMAN'S FRIEND, William Monsell, afterwards Lord Emly, had a house at Tervoe in the County Limerick countryside, which Newman borrowed for a week of rest and silence. 'The quiet set me up. It is the only thing for me ever. I have never been tired of being by myself since I was a boy.'[1]

It is thought that Newman wrote the remaining five discourses while he was at Tervoe.

Newman's Dublin discourses would ultimately be published as the brilliant classic, *The Idea of a University*, used ever since in the establishment of numerous Catholic universities worldwide.

And it is a truly beautiful book, full of inspired knowledge and wisdom, with a general sense of care and understanding for both students and their mentors. Written by this great master of stylistic prose, it has been proposed as essential reading for university students, as it aims to prepare them for life and provides answers to many of life's essential questions.

The endorsements of reviewers of this exceptional *classic* affirm its inestimable value to those who pursue a university education and also those who value the pursuit of knowledge for its own sake.

Newman would say that the collection of lectures which formed *The Idea of a University* was the most painful of all the books he wrote. They 'have oppressed me more than anything else of the kind in my life'.[2]

To Tervoe for a Rest and Silence

Notes

1   McRedmond, *Thrown among Strangers*.
2   Newman, *Letters and Diaries*, vol. 15, pp. 98–9.

✠ 16 ✠

Waiting

EWMAN HAD A LONG AND EXASPERATING WAIT before he could get his university started. During the remainder of 1852 and on into 1853 he spared no effort in making the necessary preparations. This required having to spend long periods in Dublin and away from the Birmingham Oratory, which was causing him qualms of conscience, as we see from a letter that he wrote to the Pope in 1854, close to the time of the opening of the university:

> Fr John Henry Newman ... as it is well known to your Holiness, he sustains a double charge, that of Superior of the Oratory of the Phillipine Fathers at Birmingham in England and that of Rector of the University of Dublin. As this second duty requires his services in person, and this is incompatible with his residing continuously in his house in Birmingham, therefore, to quieten his conscience, he begs Your Holiness to dispense him from the duty of such residence for some months of the year, for a period of three years.

The Pope replied: 'We concede to the Applicant that he may in all tranquillity of conscience reside in Ireland for the time required by the needs of the University' (Pius P.P. IX, 20 December 1854).[1]

AN *ANNUS HORRIBILIS*

The demands of the setting up of the university were putting Newman under considerable strain, primarily because of the travel involved in going back and forth to Ireland, but also because of the stress of the Achilli trial. Early in 1852, we note his travel arrangements for the coming months:

> Dublin early in May, back to Birmingham for a community celebration three weeks later, returning to Dublin in three days' time; to London for the Achilli trial in mid-June, to Dublin immediately after for a meeting of the University Committee; in the Oratory once more in July and on to Oscott to address there assembled bishops of England and Wales on the 'Second Spring'; to Limerick before the month was out, back to England in August to face the staggering legal costs of the trial.

Also that year his sister Harriett and much-loved aunt Elizabeth (Betsy) both died. Poor Newman, not surprisingly, collapsed while giving a talk at the Oratory in September and was warned by his doctor that he would not live long unless he moderated his pace and his activities.[2]

A WARM WELCOME IN IRELAND

Newman was amazed at the warmth of the reception in Ireland. But he was a stranger in a strange country, and sometimes he would have preferred less attention and to be left to his own company—as an ascetic and something of a recluse by nature—or at least the company of friends who would better understand the stress he was going through, primarily over the Achilli affair.

Newman had spoken out in defence of the Church and against Achilli, a renegade Italian priest, who was stirring up anti-Catholic feelings in England, by claiming that he had been held in 'horrible dungeons' by the Papal States, when in fact he had been in prison for several abuses against young girls in Italy. But he was seen as a celebrity in the then anti-Catholic England. When Newman brought the true facts to light, Achilli charged him with slander.

It was very hurtful that the Anglican Archbishop of Dublin, Whately, a friend and colleague when at Oxford, who lived quite near him in Dublin, totally ignored him when they met on the street, obviously vexed that he had become a Catholic.[3]

Newman spoke of the Oratory as his 'family' and indeed it was his haven in every storm. So in Ireland he missed the support of his Oratorian community. Also he would have missed his Oxford friends. Ireland was utterly alien in every sense to this English-born, reserved and shy man. He obviously felt lonely and isolated: 'No one knows but myself the desolateness I sustain in leaving Birmingham, and being thrown among strangers—I trust it will be taken as my penance'.[4]

Newman felt that the Irish, in what he described as their 'Ivory Tower Church', standing defiant to the infidel world where what their religion required was laid down and accepted, would have no concept of what Catholics in England, by contrast, were going through at that time. The Irish bore the marks of their history as the English bore theirs, but it was a history altogether different, however tragically intermingled with the history of Newman's countrymen.[5]

In July he was invited by Cardinal Wiseman to deliver the historic sermon at Oscott, marking the re-establishment of the diocesan episcopacy in England and Wales in 1850. It was a great honour for Newman to be invited to address this first synod of the new English hierarchy in three hundred years. Wiseman had indeed chosen the very best orator for this important occasion.

Notes

[1]   Iglesias, 'Why did Newman come to Dublin?'
[2]   McRedmond, *Thrown among Strangers*, p. 72.
[3]   *Ibid.*, p. 70.
[4]   Newman, *Letters and Diaries*, vol. 16, p. 58.
[5]   McRedmond, *Thrown among Strangers*, p. 85.

✝ 17 ✝

The Second Spring

'T HE SECOND SPRING' is recognized as Newman's best-loved sermon. In all of his writings it would be difficult to find a more beautiful portrayal of his heartfelt love for the Church than in this sermon, delivered in that 'low, sweet, unforgettable voice' from the high pulpit of Oscott's beautiful Gothic church.

In an emotional address, delivered sincerely from the heart, Newman focuses on the joy of the new 'springtime for the Church'. His enthusiasm and exuberance leaves one in no doubt as to his delight at what is happening in his 'own dear country' at this time. His beloved Church has risen from the ashes after the 'long dark winter'.

At different periods during its long history the Church has risen to the heights of its majesty and splendour and also delved to the depths of the dark night of suffering and destruction, but we were now witnessing 'the resurrection of the Church'.

> Three centuries ago, the Catholic Church, that great creation of God's power, stood in this land in pride of place. It had the honours of nearly a thousand years on it ... it was based on the will of a faithful people ... it was ennobled by a host of saints and martyrs. There were also the religious orders, its beautiful monastic establishments, its universities, its wide relations all over Europe ... all of which seemed destined to stand, so long as England stood ... But then came the long night of destruction and the martyrdoms. It took a long time to do this thoroughly; much time, much thought, much

87

> labour, much expense; but at last it was done ... Truth
> was disposed of, and shovelled away, and there was a
> calm, a silence, a sort of peace;—and such was about the
> state of things when we were born ... The old church in
> its day became a corpse ... the presence of Catholicism
> was at length simply removed.[1]

He stresses that our own English saints, whom he loves,
will help us at this time. Pointing to England's veritable
multitude of early saints, he recounts that Canterbury alone
numbered perhaps some sixteen; from St Augustine to St
Dunstan and St Elphege, from St Anselm and St Thomas
down to St Edmund. York had its St Paulinus, St John, St
Wilfrid and St William; London, its St Erconwald; Durham,
its St Cuthbert; Winchester, its St Swithun. Then there was
St Aidan of Lindisfarne, St Hugh of Lincoln, St Chad of
Lichfield, St Thomas of Hereford, and St Osmund and St
Wulfstan of Worcester, St Osmund of Salisbury, St Birinus
of Dorchester-on-Thames and St Richard of Chichester.

THE CHURCH DESTITUTE

Full of encouragement, he reminds us that the Church of
Christ will always rise from the ashes and so 'just as no one
could have prophesied its fall, so nobody could prophesy
its rise again. Its rise again was in the order of grace, who
can hope for such a miracle as this': 'Has the whole course
of history a like to show?'

Newman—ever the great encourager—expresses his
hope and trust in God and the Blessed Virgin to see them
through these storms: 'The new dawn has been born, the
winter may not yet be quite over, but whatever storms or
troubles may come, God will prevail, there would always
be springtimes of hope'.

> One thing alone I know that according to our need, so
> will be our strength. One thing I am certain of, that the
> more the enemy rages against us, so much the more

will the saints in heaven plead for us; the more fearful
are our trials from the world, the more present to us
will be our Mother Mary, and our good patrons and
Angel Guardians.

Leaving the majority of the bishops in tears, including
Wiseman, Newman places his country in the hands of the
Blessed Virgin.

O Mary, my hope, O Mother undefiled, fulfil to us the
promise of this Spring. A second temple rises on the
ruins of the old. Canterbury has gone its way, and York
is gone, and Durham is gone and Winchester is gone. It
was sore to part with them, but the church in England
has died, and the Church lives again. The martyrs did
not die in vain.

THE ACHILLI TRIAL

The stress of the impending Achilli trial — Achilli was taking
action against Newman for slander — was a huge cross for
Newman for almost two years, so he was relieved when
the day finally dawned and the trial began in London on
21 June 1852. It lasted three days. The jury brought a guilty
verdict, after a display of anti-Catholic bias by the judge,
so blatant that the strongly anti-Catholic *Times* denounced
it editorially.[2]

Cullen proved to be a good friend to Newman in this
difficulty. On 5 November the Archbishop organized a fund
to be set up for his defence at a further hearing, to which
subscriptions poured in from Irish sources, not least from
the Irish poor.[3]

'I am being killed with kindness', he wrote that summer.
'Words cannot express the exuberant hearty affection with
which all men, the priests and the multitude in the streets
embrace me.'[4]

After the Achilli trial, and pending the further hearing,
the Catholic Irish saw Newman as a walking martyr for

their religion. His lawyers moved for a new trial, so the case was not finally resolved until January 1853, without a retrial—an unbelievable moral victory for Newman but the price had been huge anxiety. He only had to pay £100, but the outcry of public sympathy he received, criticizing Judge Campbell's 'obvious bias'—which was recognized far and wide as being unjust—saw the strongly anti-Catholic *Times* reflect the mood of public sympathy. 'A great blow has been given to the administration of justice in this country, and Roman Catholics will have henceforth only too good reason for asserting that there is no justice for them in matters tending to rouse the Protestant feelings of judges and juries.'[5]

The above quotation from Newman's *Letters and Diaries* could be said to have been so positive and so supportive of the Catholic standpoint as to prove Newman's harsh approach in exposing this fraud in the public arena to be correct. For the fact that the powerfully influential *Times* expressed distaste for the verdict would have been one of the most supportive public vindications of the Catholic position ever to appear in the public press of the time.

The victory here would have been a great support for the English Catholics. Another positive outcome was that £2,000 left over from the fund organized by his defence committee was used towards the building of the new university church in Dublin and the cottage and Oratorian cemetery at Rednal.

Notes

1   Newman, 'Second Spring'.
2   McRedmond, *Thrown among Strangers*, p. 70. See also T. O'Loughlin, *Cardinal Newman, Seeker of Truth*, Dublin: Veritas, 1988, p. 18.
3   McRedmond, *Thrown among Strangers*, p. 56.
4   *Ibid.*, p. 70, to M. Johnson.
5   Newman, *Letters and Diaries*, vol. 15, p. 108.

✝ 18 ✝

A University in Preparation

I T WAS TO BE A DIFFICULT NUMBER OF YEARS before the Dublin university finally got off the ground. Delay followed delay, with important letters sent by Newman not answered by Archbishop Cullen. 'It was his rule of acting—not once, or twice, but his rule and principle—to let me ask a question in June, to call again and again ... even now in February he has not directly or indirectly, answered me.'[1]

Twice in January and February 1853 Newman wrote to the archbishop for definite instructions but again received no reply. Unknown to Newman, there was a great deal of angst on the part of Archbishop Cullen and Archbishop Mac Hale of Tuam in relation to the university, but this was not relayed to Newman, who, understandably, was very aggrieved at Cullen's behaviour; 'not to commit himself on paper; to treat me, not as an equal, but as one of his subjects'.[2]

Newman would later say that Archbishop Cullen's great fault was that 'he makes no one his friend, because he will confide in nobody, and be considerate to nobody; it was a wonder he did not "cook his own dinners", he was so distrustful of everybody'.[3]

Of interest also here is that the other 'dissident' archbishop, McHale of Tuam, when Newman met him, 'shook my hand with so violent a cordiality, when I kissed his ring, as to punish my nose'![4] This would be a very Irish way of letting Newman know that he was personally held in high esteem by the Archbishop; but this would not stop him from disagreeing with him!

Meanwhile Newman got on with the task of shaping the university, tirelessly organizing university appointments, recruiting students and staff and viewing various residences. Encouraging news came at last, this time from Rome, where Pope Pius IX had decided to issue a formal brief as the best way of starting up the university. The brief approved the appointment of Newman as rector, setting out the purpose of the university and instructing the apostolic delegates to summon a synod of bishops to agree the necessary arrangements to enable lectures to begin as early as possible.

The synod held in Dublin in May drew up a list of decrees which assumed that, in virtually all respects the university would be established and conducted on Newman's principles.[5] Whilst the bishops retained the ultimate authority, the full administrative control of the university over its academic standards and appointment of staff was vested in the rector, the exception being the appointment of the vice-rector, which was reserved to the bishops, who immediately appointed Dr Patrick Leahy of Thurles to the post.

NEWMAN TRAVELS TO IRELAND

On 7 February 1854 Newman at last set off for Dublin to set up the university. He decided, initially, on a tour of Ireland to visit the bishops and to make enquiries about the state of the colleges and schools in the country. He also wanted to spread the word in the hope of attracting potential students and teachers.

On his circuit he travelled from Kilkenny to Carlow, and from Carlow to Waterford, where he was warmly received by the bishops of both places and by the staffs of their diocesan colleges. However, he discovered that he was expected to address gatherings of priests and even pupils of a Waterford girls' school. Such impromptu invitations always left him 'groping for words'.

Newman always saw the humorous side of things and in his letters to his brothers at the Birmingham Oratory he relates a number of incidents which he found extremely amusing.

He tells of being taken by mistake to the Protestant bishop's residence by a cabbie in Kilkenny. The plaid scarf he had purchased in Dublin because of the cold indicated to the driver that he was a protestant clergyman. Fortunately, to Newman's great relief—because this bishop was no friend of his—they discovered on arriving at the house that he was away in London.

Again, he muses about falling asleep after dinner in the Carlow bishop's residence, where a group of priests had assembled to hear his plans for the proposed university.

Bishop William Delaney of Cork called with his vicar general to see Newman at the Vincentian house where he was staying in the city. His meeting with the Cork bishop, who apparently favoured the Queen's colleges, one of which had been set up in his diocese, was, to say the least, not welcoming:

> The Bishop of Cork was cold and courteous—stiff and donnish—and I should never get on with him, I am sure. He is the only bishop I have met unlike an Irishman; I think I had rather be pawed by the lion—(the lion was the 'Lion of St Jarlath's' or 'of the West')—the formidable Archbishop Mac Hale of Tuam.[6]

Two of the other Munster bishops went some way to retrieving the situation, Archbishop Slattery of Thurles he found to be 'a most pleasing, taking man—mild, gentle, tender and broken', but Bishop Ryan of Limerick made the most favourable impression on Newman. 'He is the cleverest bishop I have met, and certainly to me the kindest.'[7]

Unfortunately the country was experiencing its worst winter since 1814, and Newman, whose health was never robust, developed a bad cold, which meant he had to cut short his trip and return to Dublin. Despite the warmth of the majority of the Munster bishops, he was upset by negative comments on the university from both religious and lay quarters that 'there was simply no demand for it'. Even his friend Dr Russell looked 'despondently ... on the prospects for the university'.[8]

During his visit Newman could see for himself that post-Famine conditions added to the despondency and cited emigration and the 'ruin of families' among the factors which 'induced by centuries of oppression created the general belief that Ireland could not provide enough students to fill a Catholic university at that time'.[9] But, despite all the obstacles, he heroically, it must be said, persisted with the task of setting up his university.

Notes

1   Newman, *Letters and Diaries*, vol. 17, p. 499.
2   Newman, *Autobiographical Writings*, p. 298.
3   Newman, *Letters and Diaries*, vol. 30, p.379.
4   *Ibid.*, vol. 16, p. 172.
5   McRedmond, *Thrown among Strangers*, p. 119.
6   *Ibid.*, p. 6.
7   Newman, *Letters and Diaries*, vol. 16, p. 63.
8   McRedmond, *Thrown among Strangers*, p. 8.
9   Newman, *Letters and Diaries*, vol. 16, p. 66.

✛ 19 ✛

A Historic Day:
The Opening of Ireland's
Catholic University

O N 4 JUNE Newman was formally installed as rector by Archbishop Cullen at Dublin's pro-cathe-
dral. The big day finally came on 3 November
1854—the feast day of the great Irish saint, Malachy, and
the Catholic University under its first rector, John Henry
Newman, officially opened at 86 St Stephen's Green with an
international gathering of some twenty registered students
from Ireland, England, France and Scotland.

Newman told his small group that they would look back
on this day with great pride when they were old, citing his
now famous prophecy and challenge for the university:

> I look towards a land both old and young; old in its
> Christianity, young in the promise of its future ... I
> contemplate a people which has had a long night, and
> will have an inevitable day. I am turning my eyes towards
> a hundred years to come, and I dimly see the island I
> am gazing on become the road of passage and union
> between two hemispheres, and the centre of the world
> ... The capital of that prosperous and hopeful land is
> situate in a beautiful bay and near a romantic region;
> and in it I see a flourishing university, which for a
> while had to struggle with fortune, but which, when
> its first founders and servants were dead and gone, had
> successes far exceeding their anxieties.[1]

On 9 November the first rector (president) of the Catholic University of Dublin gave his inaugural address on 'Christianity and Letters' in the newly established School of Philosophy and Letters.

STUDENT RESIDENCES

Newman's idea was that students should stay in independent, self-supporting halls or colleges under a dean with resident tutors, who would represent 'that union of intellectual and moral influence, the separation of which is the evil of the age'.[2] Each house would have its own chapel and common table.

The university consequently opened with three houses: The first was at 86 St Stephen's Green, then known as St Patrick's or University House, the second at 16 Harcourt Street, known as St Lawrence's, and the third, under Newman's personal supervision, was at 6 Harcourt Street, known as St Mary's.

The following year the Medical School was opened on 10 October 1855 in a handsome building acquired by Newman at Cecilia Street, with a well-equipped library of over 5,000 volumes.

During that year Newman drew up the rules and regulations of the university. He had a fully developed scheme for segmenting the study-course. The first two years would be spent on basic humanities such as Latin, Greek, logic and mathematics. Students leaving after this would have a grounding in liberal education, certified by the degree of Scholar.

Those who remained for another two years would concentrate on specific subjects, some of them of a quasi-professional nature: metaphysics, economics, law, history. They would qualify for the degree of Batchelor. Three more years would lead to post-graduate degrees — Master of Letters or Science; Doctor of Theology, Law or Medicine.[3]

NEWMAN'S AIM AS RECTOR INCLUDES REACHING OUT TO THE COMMUNITY

Newman believed in the important role the laity must play in the management and teaching of the university. His idea of appointing lay professors was met with a great deal of disapproval initially by Cullen and some of the bishops, who thought the staff of a Catholic university should all be priests. Despite these objections, Newman persisted in instating a talented staff of primarily lay professors.

For Newman, who always believed in personal contact, the 'great instrument, or rather organ' of a university is 'the personal presence of a teacher'.[4] 'An academic system without the personal influence of teachers upon pupils is an "arctic winter"; it will create an ice-bound, petrified, cast-iron university.'[5]

Newman realized that it was important to 'make a show' in order to provide a high profile for the university.[6] So he determined to appoint distinguished and well-known professors, who would draw students to the university. He aimed to appoint Catholic professors, Irishmen wherever possible, but not to hesitate to appoint Englishmen when academic priorities justified it.

Appointments included Eugene O'Curry—chair of archaeology and Irish history; John O'Hagan—political economy, Aubrey de Vere—political and social science. The three professors of theology were appointed by the hierarchy; Newman had handed over responsibility for theology to the Irish hierarchy.

The first named student on the list was the grandson of Daniel O'Connell, the liberator. Among the eight students accommodated at Newman's own house were a French viscount, an Irish baronet, the son of a French countess, the grandson of a Scottish marquess and the son of an English lord. Later two Belgian princes and a Polish count were added.

Newman saw in this Catholic University a continuation of the Oxford Movement: amongst the non-Irish students many were the sons of friends who had been influenced by the Oxford Movement. Also some of his professors and benefactors were converts, so to a certain extent the Catholic University was linked to the Oxford Movement.[7]

The helpful advice offered to students by Newman's well-known maxim 'A little, but well', is as relevant today as it was when he wrote it in the 1850s:

> A little, but well ... that is, really know what you say you know: know what you know and what you do not know; get one thing well before you go on to a second; try to ascertain what your words mean; when you read a sentence, picture it before your mind as a whole, take in the truth or information contained in it, express it in your own words, and, if it be important, commit it to the faithful memory. Again, compare one idea with another; adjust truths and facts; form them into one whole, or notice the obstacles which occur in doing so. This is the way to make progress; this is the way to arrive at results; not to swallow knowledge, but (according to the figure sometimes used) to masticate and digest it.[8]

Newman wanted the students to have a balanced approach to university life and study, and to enjoy the experience. And so he provided a billiard table and allowed them to go hunting and to the theatre. In contrast, some of the bishops thought the university should be run on the lines of a seminary, allowing very little freedom to the students.

The Medical School, set up by Newman and opened in 1855 in Cecilia Street, is the Catholic University's great success story. By the end of the century it had become the largest medical school in the country. In 1908 it became the medical faculty of University College Dublin and remains as such to this day.

Before Newman established the Medical School, out of 111 doctors in situations of authority in Dublin's five medical schools and hospitals, twelve were Catholic and ninety-nine Protestant.

Notes

1   McCartney, *University College Dublin*, p. 12.
2   Newman, *My Campaign in Ireland*, pp. 39, 120.
3   McRedmond, *Thrown among Strangers*, p. 121.
4   Newman, *Historical Sketches*, vol. 3, pp. 14, 74–5.
5   *Ibid.*, p. 14.
6   Newman, *Letters and Diaries*, vol. 16. 155.
7   McCartney, *University College Dublin*, p. 6.
8   Newman, *Apologia.*

University Church Dublin, Our Lady Seat of Wisdom

*I trust we shall put ourselves under
the patronage of the Sedes Sapientiae.*[1]

T HE NEXT STOP is on our pilgrim journey is the beautiful university church dedicated to Our Lady Seat of Wisdom on St Stephen's Green, Dublin, which was founded by Cardinal Newman for his Catholic University. In planning his proposed university, Newman saw a university church as his first priority.

The church would primarily symbolize 'the great principle of the university, the indissoluble union of philosophy and religion'. On a practical level it would provide a setting for university sermons. It would also prove to be valuable as providing a suitable location for the formal and public acts of the university—conferring of degrees, solemn lectures and addresses on important occasions. For such occasions it would provide a place 'ennobled by the religious symbols which were its furniture'.

Tucked between two more majestic buildings, this little 'jewel-box' of a church's red-brick façade has none of the splendour of number 86, Newman House, next door, but its entrance is an essential part of its charm. It announces its presence on St Stephen's Green with a church notice board with one of Cardinal Newman's best-loved reflections:

> May He support us all the day long, till the shades
> lengthen, and the evening comes, and the busy world

is hushed, and the fever of life is over, and our work is
done! Then in His mercy may He give us safe lodging,
and a holy rest, and peace at the last!

This beautiful legacy of a church that Newman left to Ireland is neo-Byzantine in style, built with the £2,000 left
over from the Achilli trial. Despite lack of money and lack
of space, Newman was determined to use every possible
means to create a spectacularly beautiful church, which he
would later describe as 'the most beautiful one in the three
kingdoms'.

In Milan when visiting churches, Newman had admitted
to preferring the 'brightness, grace, and simplicity of the
classical style'.

> My heart has ever gone with Grecian. I loved Trinity
> Chapel at Oxford more than any other building. There
> is in the Italian style such a simplicity, purity, elegance,
> beauty, brightness, which I suppose the word 'classical'
> implies, that it seems to befit the notion of an Angel
> or Saint.[2]

The talented Oxford artist, John Hungerford Pollen, was
recommended to Newman, who wrote to Pollen offering
him the post of 'Fine Arts Professor' at his new university
and also a commission to help with the decoration of the
university church. At Oxford Pollen had decorated the roof
of St Peter-le-Bailey (the church where he was the curate)
and also the chapel roof at Merton College (where he was
a Fellow).

These two men had never met, but Pollen, who was
twenty years younger than Newman and who was also
a convert to Catholicism, had a huge regard for him and
knew of his reputation from Oxford. Both had suffered as a
consequence of becoming Catholic. Pollen lost his financial
legacy from an uncle, and lost his position at Oxford too.

In Newman and Pollen a meeting of minds took place.
Both had a love of Byzantine art and architecture and both
considered St Mark's in Venice as 'the most wonderful
building', far exceeding St Peter's:

Basilican buildings exhibited 'elements of consummate grandeur', Pollen declared, but they needed 'the help of colour' and 'colour is like melody'.

For Pollen, the basilican style of Newman's church made its impact entirely through interior arrangements. The severe limitations of the site could easily be adapted to his design proposals, though the basic ideas for the church came from Newman.

The entrance porch leads to a passage-way running between numbers 87 and 86 St Stephen's Green on to the main body of the church. Once inside, the atmosphere of the Italian basilicas is irresistibly evoked in this crypt-like 'ante-chapel', as Pollen called it.

The floor of the sanctuary is raised above the level of the nave, and in front of the steps up from the nave is a short alabaster communion rail. An unusual feature of the sanctuary is a small choir-gallery which flanks one side of it. The idea of providing such a gallery was Newman's own, and would have been linked with his love of liturgical music.

Writing to F. S. Bowles 23 June 1855, he explains that the first item he thought of providing for the church was an organ: 'My dear Frederic', he wrote, 'will you tell me what sort of an organ you would recommend me to get ... for £250'.

Newman travelled especially to Rome, commissioning large copies of Raphael's masterpieces to be hung on the upper walls of the church. He was determined to use local craftsmen, to show Irish capabilities, and local materials wherever possible. Consequently he sourced marble from all over Ireland, at 'immense expense': greens from Galway, reds from Cork, greys and browns from Laois (Queen's County) and Armagh and the famous black marble from Kilkenny.

The work of traditional Dublin craftsmanship, in stone-cutting, wood-carving and carpentry, displays not only extraordinary talent, but the love and reverence of the craftsmen for their work.

Anyone visiting this beautiful church today should take note of the six tall Byzantine-style candlesticks on the altar. These are made, not of metal as they appear to be, which Newman could not afford, but of wood, gilded to look like metal. It is hard to believe that these were carved by the carpenters employed on the site. These and the other excellent 'spirited' wood and stone carving in the University Church were crafted by ordinary workmen. The alabaster capitals of the pillars supporting the choir-gallery are also fine examples of this carving.

'The more I looked at the apse', Newman remarked to Pollen, 'the more beautiful it seemed to me — and to my taste, the church is the most beautiful one in the three kingdoms.'[3]

This beautiful church was consecrated on 1 May 1856, the feast of the Ascension. In his first sermon preached here, entitled 'Intellect, the Instrument of Religious Training', Newman contends:

> Some persons will say that I am thinking of confining, distorting, and stunting the growth of the intellect by ecclesiastical supervision. I have no such thought. Devotion is not a sort of finish given to the sciences, nor is science a sort of feather in the cap, if I may express myself, an ornament and set-off to devotion. I want the intellectual layman to be religious, and the devout ecclesiastic to be intellectual.

Very well attended today, and very much appreciated for its beauty, the church is particularly popular for weddings. Newman's famous commentary on the laity is framed in the church porch.

In later life, Newman's friend and constant companion, Fr William Neville, wrote, 'There are not many now alive who can have any idea of the anxiety which this Church brought upon him'.[4]

The day Newman left Dublin for good, 4 November 1858, he delivered his farewell lecture, 'Christianity and Medical Science', to a packed audience in the University Church. It is a summing up of his mission to Dublin:

Though this University and Faculty of Medicine which belongs to it are as yet only in the commencement of their long career of usefulness, yet while I live, and (I trust) after life, it will be ever a theme of thankfulness for my heart and lips, that I have been allowed to do even a little, and to witness so much, of the arduous, pleasant, and hopeful toil which has attended on their establishment.

Ireland owes an immense debt of gratitude to Cardinal Newman for this beautiful church, but also to the artist, Pollen—these two converts to Catholicism—whose genius generously contributed to bringing to life this truly beautiful University Church.

Notes

1   Newman, *Letters and Diaries*, vol. 16, 144.
2   *Ibid.*, vol. 11, p. 246.
3   *Ibid.*, vol. 17, p. 440.
4   Newman, *My Campaign in Ireland*, p. 308.

✠ 21 ✠

Prayer Life

If you cannot pray, pray.
St Francis de Sales

W HEN NEWMAN recommends that his university students should have God in their lives,
he leads by example. Prayer constituted the
spiritual texture of Newman's life from his childhood on,
the Newman scholar, Dr P. Boyce, asserts. Newman's faith
in God was 'vibrant and certain . . . It was the absolute cer-
tainty of an honest lover of truth. It was on his firm faith
that his prayer was grounded.'[1]

Even as a child Newman was composing prayers; the
fathers of the Birmingham Oratory have several books of his
well-thumbed prayers. His private journals also have lists of
prayers and petitions used by him from his teenage years.
Therefore, when he became a Catholic, he did not have to
learn to pray: prayer was a habit already acquired. What he
did add were prayers to the intercession of the saints and to
the Blessed Virgin, the Rosary and prayer before the Blessed
Sacrament, which he was totally devoted to.[2]

At Oriel College he made a little private oratory from a
closet close to his rooms, where he had a crucifix and pic-
tures of his favourite saints on the wall. He would spend
long hours at prayer there. He always had a picture of St
Francis de Sales over his writing desk. This patron of writers
and journalists was his favourite saint.

Newman teaches that prayer cannot be separated from
the way we live our lives. The sincerity of our prayer has

to be visible in the Christian witness we put into practice in our daily lives, in our everyday conduct.

> Beware lest your religion be one of sentiment merely, not of practice. Men may speak in a high imaginative way of the ancient saints and the Holy Apostolic Church, without making the fervour or refinement of their devotion bear upon their conduct. Many a man likes to be religious in graceful language; he loves religious tales and hymns, yet is never the better Christian for all this.[3]

Newman always prayed in a simple and natural fashion, and this is the approach to prayer that he encourages; just talk to God as you would to a friend. 'Prayer is simply man's conversation with his God and Creator.'

He shunned mystical eloquence and preferred 'real words, real sentiments, real decisions, humble and commonplace as they might be, to the apparently rapturous artificial language of insincerity. He let the words he penned be the expression of what he genuinely felt.'[4]

He was wary of sentimental devotion and did not agree with those who, in order to pray, thought they had to stimulate their feelings and work themselves into a state of raised emotions. Newman stresses that 'those who look for an emotional experience will never attain to a life of genuine prayer'. Perseverance at prayer is very important—don't give up. 'We ought always to pray and not lose heart' (Luke 18:1). 'Faith, not feelings', for Newman, 'was the simple and sure means of contacting Christ. It may not always be an easy self-satisfying path, but to think that we can improve it by the introduction of feelings and ideas of our own is a great yet common mistake.'[5]

For true faith is 'colourless, like air or water', but many are tempted to substitute 'a feeling notion, sentiment, conviction or act of reason', which they may hang over, and dote upon. They rather aim at experiences (as they are called) within them, than at Him that is without them.[6]

Cardinal Newman's understanding was that faith is passed on not *en masse*, but in personal contact, whether it is through the written word or by some other means. Newman often speaks of this, and it goes well with his motto, 'Heart speaks to heart', that personal contact is what is necessary for evangelization and for the faith to be passed on.

Notes

1   P. Boyce, OCD, *At Prayer with John Henry Newman*. Rome: International Centre of Newman Friends, 2007, p. 4.
2   *Ibid.*, pp. 5–6.
3   Newman, *Parochial and Plain Sermons*, vol. 1, p. 51.
4   Boyce, *At Prayer*, p. 9.
5   *Ibid.*
6   Newman, *Lectures on the Doctrine of Justification*; also Boyce, *At Prayer*, p. 9.

✠ 22 ✠

✠ 22 ✠

Tributes to the Catholic University's First President

THE CATHOLIC UNIVERSITY
HONOURS ITS FIRST PRESIDENT

O N 25 March 1879 the Irish Members of Parliament wrote a letter to congratulate Newman on being elected cardinal, expressing their profound gratitude for his contribution to the Catholic University of Dublin.

Newman travelled expressly to London to receive this commendation. He responded:

> I first went over to Ireland with a view to that engagement which I afterwards formed there, and during the seven years through which that engagement lasted I had a continued experience of kindness, and nothing but kindness from all classes of people: from the hierarchy, from the seculars and regulars, and from the laity, whether in Dublin or in the country. As their first act they helped me in a great trouble in which I was involved. I had put my foot into an unusual legal embarrassment, and it required many thousands of pounds to draw me out of it. They took a great share in that work. Nor did they show less kindness at the end of my time. I was obliged to leave Ireland by the necessities of my own Congregation at Birmingham ... Not a word of disappointment or unkindness was uttered, when there might have been a feeling that I was relinquishing a work which I had begun.

The parchment which is the record of your generosity shall be committed to our archives, and shall testify to generations to come the enduring kindness of Catholics towards the founder of the first head of the English Oratory.

A further handsome tribute to Newman's contribution to the Catholic University sits in the Newman Archives in Birmingham. This beautiful Irish document, written on vellum, was sent to Cardinal Newman on 20 May 1879, years after his departure from Ireland. This document from the 'Catholic University of Ireland, Bono Club' was sent to congratulate Newman on becoming a cardinal. It is signed by the honorary secretaries of the club, William Dillon and H. J. Gill. It states:

> We have found in your writings a never-failing counsel and guidance ... we can never forget that the Lectures on the Scope and Nature of University Education were delivered in our halls and by our Rector ... the Catholics of this country, having been for three centuries excluded from all share in the advantages of higher education, had no traditions to guide them in forming a correct estimate of what a university ought to be. Your great work, which we may justly call our Charter, has supplied the place of those traditions, and thanks to it, the Irish people have now realized what a true university should be ... and what inestimable benefit [it] could confer upon Ireland.

In the following tribute by John Hungerford Pollen, professor of fine arts at the university and architect of the University Church, we catch a glimpse of the esteem in which Newman was held by his university staff in Dublin:

> He shed cheerfulness as a sunbeam sheds light, even while many difficulties were pressing. Delightful it was to be on his staff, and to hear him draw out, with the gentlest possible forceps, what each friend or professor had to say on his own particular theme ... all this under the form of easy conversation'.

John O'Hagan, a young Irelander and the professor of political economy at the university, wrote that 'so far as regards the Irish Professors in the University ... we have always felt that you only wanted power and freedom of action to make the institution march'.[1]

Newman saw his aim as rector was not only to raise the educational standard of Catholics, but also to reach out to the community. As Wilfred Ward writes, 'It is clear that the idea of the university as an intellectual and spiritual centre was prominent on his mind, and that he thought of its influence on society at large as well as on its alumni'. Dr McCartney, Professor Emeritus of University College Dublin, writes:

> In all he has bequeathed — whether by way of the buildings in St Stephen's Green, in which he laboured, or the ideas incorporated in his legacy, or the vision he handed on, or the challenges he posed — Newman has forever left UCD in particular and university education in general in his debt.[2]

The Catholic University was unique not only in having as its first president a person who became a candidate for sainthood (now a saint), but also in being the only university in Ireland or Britain financed by the pennies of the poor.[3]

Notes

1   Newman, *Letters and Diaries*, vol. 18.
2   McCartney, *University College Dublin*, p. 12.
3   *Ibid.*

✢ 23 ✢

Newman and the Role of the Laity

S T JOHN HENRY NEWMAN was ahead of his time in recognizing the important role of the laity in the Church, which is one reason why he has been called 'a prophet of the Second Vatican Council'. Vatican II's 'Decree on the Apostolate of Lay People', *Apostolicam Actuositatem*, 18 November 1965, confirmed Newman's thinking on the important role of the laity in the Church.

> I want a laity, not arrogant, not rash in speech, not disputatious, but men who know their religion, who enter into it, who know just where they stand, who know what they hold and what they do not, who know their creed so well that they can give an account of it, who know so much of history that they can defend it. I want an intelligent, well-instructed laity—I wish you to enlarge your knowledge, to cultivate your reason, to get an insight into the relation of truth to truth, to learn to view things as they are, to understand how faith and reason stand to each other, what are the bases and principles of Catholicism and where lies the main inconsistencies and absurdities of the Protestant theory.
>
> I have no apprehension you will be the worse Catholics for familiarity with these subjects, provided you cherish a vivid sense of God above and keep in mind that you have souls to be judged and saved. In all times the laity have been the measure of the Catholic spirit; they saved the Irish Church three centuries ago ... You ought to be able to bring out what you feel and what you mean, as well as to feel and mean it; to expose to the comprehension of others the fictions and fallacies of

> your opponents; to explain the charges brought against
> the Church, to the satisfaction, not, indeed, of bigots,
> but of men of sense, of whatever cast of opinion.[1]

The sentiment expressed in this reflection, which today sits in the porch of Newman's University Church in College Green in Dublin, is presented as a challenge to the evening students, when 'their Rector' addressed them shortly before leaving Ireland and his beloved university for the last time.

Newman has further advice for those who wish to live a good Christian life:

> If you ask me what you are to do in order to be perfect, I say, first: Do not lie in bed beyond the due time of rising; give your first thoughts to God; make a good visit to the Blessed Sacrament; say the Angelus devoutly; eat and drink to God's glory; say the Rosary well; be recollected; keep out bad thoughts; make your evening meditation well; examine yourself daily; go to bed in good time, and you are already perfect.[2]

ADDRESS TO EVENING STUDENTS

On 26 October 1858 Newman travelled to Dublin for the last time.

Newman was ahead of his time in launching a system of evening lectures for students who were working during the day, before any other college in the country. The ninety or so students — with some females among them — who attended the evening classes gathered that evening for a last address from their beloved Rector.

Newman decided 'it was a great thing to employ the time of young men of an evening', and that 'it was better they should be awake or asleep in a lecture room, than in many other places which they might otherwise frequent'.[3]

Initially the evening classes were slow to get off the ground and had to be discontinued for a time, but at this stage they had become very popular and well attended. His discourse that evening, entitled 'Discipline of Mind', was a poignant plea to 'these young men of Dublin' to use their education to play their crucial role in 'that great work, which is now so fully before the public'.[4]

As he addressed those 'sleepy inattentive evening students', it is evident that Newman had familiarized himself, if he needed to, with the state of things in Ireland which he pleaded ignorance of when he presented his first lecture at the Rotunda seven years before.

He tells them that when he became a Catholic one of his first questions was 'Why have not our Catholics a university?' He believed, he said, that 'Ireland, and the metropolis of Ireland, was obviously the proper seat of such an institution'. On account of Ireland's 'ancient hereditary Catholicity, and of the future which is in store for it, it is impossible, gentlemen, to doubt that a future is in store for Ireland, for more reasons than can here be enumerated'.[5]

There are many incidents that show how Newman made every effort to help the people of the country where his university was planted. We note his concern in this regard as he sets this challenge before the 'young men of Dublin' that evening, specially taking the time to address them before leaving Ireland:

> much I desire that this university should be of service to the young men of Dublin. I do not desire this benefit to you, simply for your own sakes. For your own sakes certainly I wish it, but not on your own account only ... You are born for Ireland; and, in your advancement, Ireland is advanced; — in your advancement in what is good and what is true, in knowledge, in learning, in cultivation of mind, in enlightened attachment to your religion, in good name and respectability and social influence.[6]

With the perception of the prophet, Newman advises the students that their knowledge and their faith will be needed... 'when a subtle logic is used against the Church, and demands a logic, still more subtle on the part of her defenders to expose it'.[7]

> There will ever be a number of persons ... too young to be wise, too generous to be cautious, too warm to be sober, or too intellectual to be humble. Such persons will be very apt to attach themselves to particular persons, to use particular names, to say things merely because others do and to act in a party spirited way.[8]

Notes

1. Newman, lecture 9 of *The Present Position of Catholics in England*.
2. Newman, *Meditations and Devotions*.
3. Newman, *Letters and Diaries*, vol. 18, p. 263.
4. 'Discipline of Mind. An Address to the Evening Classes', in *The Idea of a University*, no. 9.
5. *Ibid.*
6. *Ibid.*
7. *Ibid.*
8. Newman, *Apologia*.

✛ 24 ✛

Leaving Dublin

WHEN NEWMAN left Dublin on 4 November 1858, he had crossed the Irish Sea 56 times in seven years in the service of the university, even though he hated travelling. He offered his resignation on 12 November, seven years to the day since his appointment as Rector.

His resignation was not surprising. In his resignation letter Newman had included a reference to his doctor's fear that he had heart-trouble and had to avoid anxiety.

Archbishop Leahy, then vice-rector, had written to ask Newman to spend more time in Dublin in the coming year, even suggesting that the Birmingham Oratory or part of it, which he considered 'dwindles ... to a small thing in comparison with the Catholic University', be moved to Dublin to accommodate Newman's much-needed, on-going contribution to the university, for which 'it is my belief that providence was preparing you long years before your secession from the Church of England'.[1]

Newman gave the principal reason for retiring as 'the fatigue of journeying between Birmingham and Dublin', but it was because he could not comply with Cullen's request to take up permanent residency as he was needed at the Birmingham Oratory.[2]

Most of the bishops responded warmly, regretting his decision to leave and fearing for the future of the university. Newman did not want to leave altogether, if he could revert to the position of Prefect of Studies, which he had wanted initially. He was obviously broken-hearted at the idea of withdrawing from his beloved university. He had more work to do.

His memories of Ireland were very pleasant, apart from his treatment by Cullen and MacHale. But in the following comment we note the trial it was for him to move from his Oratorian brothers and his Birmingham Oratory: 'it was a mortification . . . to separate myself from persons I love so much and from a work to which all my human feelings so much incline me'. But in summary, Newman contends that 'On the whole there had been the most perfect harmony.'[3]

On 1 January 1858 the first number of the new university journal, *Atlantis*, which he set up, was published, with Newman contributing an article on monastic education, and several other articles in later editions. He hoped that the journal would 'act as considerable advertisement and pull'.[4] Also he thought that the journal would be one way in which he could keep up a connection with the university. It was to appear twice a year and to contain research in the arts and sciences, but not specifically theology proper.[5]

Notes

[1]   Newman, *Letters and Diaries*, vol. 18, p. 478.
[2]   *Ibid.*, p. 9.
[3]   *Ibid.*, p. 214.
[4]   *Ibid.*, p. 218.
[5]   *Ibid.*

✛ 25 ✛

Newman's Legacy
to his Dublin University

A T HIS UNIVERSITY Newman founded a chair of poetry and one of the first chairs of English literature in Ireland or Britain. His university was also at the forefront of European academic advancement, with chairs of political and social science, political economy and geography. He also founded the first chair of archaeology and Irish history in Ireland.[1]

The Catholic University's first Rector also founded the Literary, Historical and Aesthetical Society, now called the Literary and Historical Society, for discussion and debate. Newman's cardinal motto, *Cor ad cor loquitur*, continues to this day as the motto of the society.

Note

[1]   McCartney, *University College Dublin*, p. 12.

✣ 26 ✣

Augustine Birrell's Bill of 1908

THE IRISH UNIVERSITIES BILL of 1908 introduced by Augustine Birrell—British Chief Secretary—was steered skilfully through Parliament and became law as the Irish Universities Act on 1 August 1908.

This was the statute that brought into being the National University of Ireland, with its administrative centre in Dublin and its constituent university colleges (so termed) in Dublin, Cork and Galway. Sadly, it brought about the demise of Newman's then Jesuit-run Catholic University.

The premises in St Stephen's Green—the 'flagship' of the Catholic University—were to be the first home of the New University College, rented from the Jesuits.

Birrell also determined that the first head of the Dublin institution should be a layman. The new colleges were to be non-denominational. The Cecilia Street Medical School was to become the Medical Faculty of University College Dublin.

The Catholic bishops accepted the new Act without enthusiasm, but also without overt opposition, except for Bishop Edward O'Dwyer of Limerick, who felt it did not give them enough. Trinity College, Dublin, was not affected by this legislation.[1]

> Nothing would be done at all if one waited until one could do it so well that no one could find fault with it.[2]

Prof. Emerita Teresa Iglesias, founding director of the International Centre for Newman Studies at UCD, relates that:

The university Newman governed and left behind was constituted by two major university houses, three faculties, Letters, Science and Medicine, a professional body of 23 members with their assisting lectures and tutors, over a hundred students and a University Church, claiming that: 'Such an institution will give unity to the various academic functions . . . it will maintain and symbolize the great principle in which we glory as our characteristic, the union of Science with Religion.'

'THERE'S A SAINT IN THAT MAN'

In a letter to Newman on 2 June 1864, Bishop Ullathorne of Birmingham congratulated him on his great work of establishing the Congregation of the Oratory of St Philip Neri in both London and Birmingham, and on the founding of the Catholic University in Dublin.

> No sooner was this work fairly on foot than you were called by the highest authority to commence another, and one of yet greater magnitude and difficulty, the founding of a university in Ireland. After the universities had been lost to the Catholics of these kingdoms for three centuries, everything had to be begun from the beginning: the idea of such an institution to be inculcated, the plan to be formed that would work; the resources to be gathered, and the staff of superiors and professors to be brought together. Your name was then the chief point of attraction which brought these elements together. You alone know what difficulties you had to conciliate and what to surmount, before the work reached that state of consistency and promise, which enabled you to return to those responsibilities in England which you had never laid aside or suspended.

In a lovely image Bishop Ullathorne further relates:

> I was lately reading a poem, not long published, from the MSS. *De Rerum Natura*, by Neckham, the foster-brother of Richard the Lionhearted. He quotes an old prophecy attributed to Merlin, and with a sort of wonder, as if

recollecting that England owed so much of its literary learning to that country, and the prophecy says that after long years Oxford will pass to Ireland—'Vada boum suo tempore transibunt in Hiberniam [Oxford in its time will pass over to Ireland].' When I read this, I could not but indulge the pleasant fancy that in the days when the Dublin University shall arise in material splendour, an allusion to this prophecy might form a poetic element in the inscription on the pedestal of the statue which commemorates its first Rector.[3]

Notes

[1]   The above information is taken from McCartney, *University College Dublin*, pp. 26–7.

[2]   Newman, 'Developing the Leader within You', lecture 9 in *The Present Position of Catholics in England*.

[3]   Newman, *Apologia*.

Rome

NEWMAN'S FIRST VISIT TO ROME

NEWMAN MADE FOUR VISITS during his life to Rome, which mark major landmarks on his journey towards the Catholic Church.

When he first visited the Eternal City in the spring of 1833, he was on a Mediterranean steamship tour with his friend Hurrell Froude and Froude's father. At the time Newman was a young Oxford don and a priest of the Anglican Church with an abhorrence of Roman Catholicism.

On their first day they paid a visit to the English College, the *Venerabile Collegio Inglese*, where they met the Rector, Monsignor (later) Cardinal Wiseman—who was later to play such a major role in Newman's life. But on the whole during that visit they 'kept clear of Catholics'.[1] They did meet the Dean of Malta and had a conversation with him about the Church Fathers and the library of the great church of Alexandria.

He writes of his first experience of Rome: 'Rome is a very difficult place to speak of from the mixture of good and evil in it—the heathen state was accursed ... and the Christian system there is deplorably corrupt—yet the dust of the Apostles lies there and the present clergy are their descendants'.[2]

He was angry, coming from the Anglican tradition, at what he saw as elaborate manifestations of anti-Christian features in what he calls 'the Roman system' of the Catholic

Church: the pomp, the show, the luxurious altar dressings and vestments, the appearance of the Sovereign Pontiff and of the religious 'court of Rome'. 'When I was young ... and after I was grown up, I thought the Pope to be Antichrist. At Christmas 1824–5 I preached a sermon to that effect.'[3]

Froude, who was very Catholic in his thinking, helped him to grow 'less and less bitter' towards the Church of Rome on that visit.

Newman was fascinated to find that many of the ancient pagan buildings, such as the Pantheon and the baths of Diocletian, had been turned into churches.[4] Buildings such as the Colosseum did upset him, however, 'at the thought of the purposes to which they were dedicated'.[5] Yet he marvelled at the exceptional beauty of the eternal city; the examples of ancient sculpture and of Renaissance painting; the beauty of the churches; the splendid bridges and the fountains captivated him. In the many letters he wrote to friends and family at the time, he declares that 'Rome ... is of all cities the first, and ... all I ever saw are but as dust, even dear Oxford inclusive, compared with the majesty and glory ... Rome grows more wonderful every day.'[6]

SECOND VISIT TO ROME

On Newman's second visit he was accompanied by Ambrose St John; they spent five weeks in Milan *en route* before arriving in Rome on 28 October 1846. This was just over a year since he had entered the Roman Catholic Church, having resigned as vicar of the University Church of St Mary the Virgin and moved to Maryvale.

It is thought that it was at this time, overwhelmed by the beauty of Milan's *duomo*, that Newman wrote his famous account of the beauty of a Catholic cathedral:

> A Catholic cathedral is a sort of world, every one going about his own business, but that business a religious one; groups of worshippers, and solitary ones—kneeling,

standing—some at shrines, some at altars—hearing
Mass and communicating—currents of worshippers
intercepting and passing by each other—altar after
altar lit up for worship, like stars in the firmament—or
the bell giving notice of what is going on in parts you
do not see—and all the while the Canons in the choir
going through matins and lauds, and at the end of it
the incense rolling up from the high altar, and all this
in one of the most wonderful buildings in the world
and every day—lastly, all of this without any show or
effort, but what everyone is used to—everyone at his
own work, and leaving everyone else to his.[7]

This second journey to Rome was to study for the Catholic priesthood at the Collegium de Propaganda Fide, thus
marking an extraordinary change in his life and thinking
from that first visit with Hurrell Forde thirteen years earlier.
'To live is to change, to be perfect is to have changed often'.[8]

On their first morning in Rome they went to St Peter's
to recite the Apostles' Creed at the tomb of St Peter. Going
to the Vatican as soon as arriving in Rome to profess their
faith at this central home of Christianity shows how much
in tune they were with their Catholic faith. What took place
there was providential, as Newman writes: 'and there was
the Pope, at the tomb saying Mass—so that he was the
first person I saw in Rome ... This was an extraordinary
happening because apparently nobody knew the Pope was
there that morning, he had gone in private.'[9]

They were treated like 'princes' at the Propaganda, all their
needs looked after. But it was difficult for this former Anglican
priest to be a seminarian with all the young seminarians at
the college. After a time he and St John stopped attending
lectures and read in their room instead. As he writes, he was
not young any more, but 'so stiff and wooden'.[10]

Newman mentions in his letters that their windows at
the Propaganda looked down on the church of Sant' Andrea
delle Fratte, where a miracle had taken place on 20 January 1842, when Our Lady of the Miraculous Medal had
appeared to Alphonse Ratisbonne.[11]

On this visit to Rome, Newman had a great appreciation of the 'Real Presence' in the churches, and the sense of
warmth of the churches with their sanctuary lamps welcoming all to the Divine Presence. 'It is really most wonderful to see the Divine Presence looking out almost into
the open streets from the various churches ... I never knew
what worship was, as an objective fact, till I entered the
Catholic Church.'[12]

He was shocked by the poor state of both philosophy
and theology at the Propaganda. There was no study of
Aristotle or of St Thomas Aquinas. On this visit to Rome
Newman and St John had the privilege of being invited to
visit Pope Pius IX.

They had to decide what religious congregation to join,
and settled on the Oratorians because of its sixteenth-cen-
tury founder St Philip Neri, but also because the Oratorian
life was what they wanted. It was Wiseman who suggested
the Oratorians—a community of secular priests living under
a rule but not under vows; the Oratory of St Philip Neri
offered a middle way between a religious order and the
diocesan priesthood.

The Oratory also offered opportunities for learning
and scholarship, as well as for active pastoral work. The
Oratory idea was flexible enough to admit of a variety of
possibilities.[13] So they went to visit the Roman Oratory
and decided that this was the religious congregation they
wished to join.

On Newman's forty-sixth birthday, 21 February 1847,
Pope Pius IX appointed him to introduce St Philip's Oratory to England. He offered the monastery of Santa Croce
in Gerusalemme to the future English congregation for the
first part of their noviciate from July to December 1847.[14]

On Trinity Sunday, 30 May 1847, Cardinal Fransoni
ordained Newman, St John, and some of their fellow converts from Maryvale, as priests at the Propaganda College.
'All the students of the college were present and they had
the organ play.'[15]

Afterwards they went to visit Santa Croce. On 28 June they moved there to begin their formation as Oratorians. In the evening they all walked to St Peter's in thanksgiving.

On their return journey to England the group stopped at Loretto to place their congregation under the protection of the Blessed Virgin Mary.

And so on returning from Rome in 1847, Newman was an Oratorian priest and superior of the English Oratory. One of the first Masses he said in England was at Warwick Street in London, where today the Ordinariate has its headquarters. Newman had been there as a young boy in 1811 with his father, who had wanted to hear a particular piece of music being sung.

THIRD VISIT TO ROME

The purpose of Newman's third visit to Rome, in the company of Ambrose St John again, was to solve some problems which had developed between the two houses in England involving Faber and his group concerning the interpretation of the Oratorian rule.

For Newman it was a 'business of very great anxiety', and he and St John decided that they should offer up a severe penance for their Oratory. This they did by walking barefoot over the stones in the depths of winter on 13 January 1856, their long Propaganda cloaks hiding their bare feet. They then went to pray at the tomb of St Peter.

Thankfully the trip defused the problems in England, as the Holy Father granted them 'whatever they asked for', and more. Consequently the two Oratories in London and Birmingham became independent. Newman would not allow any gossip to damage the London Oratory. Faber and friends were doing good work and he left them to do it in their own way.

His four visits to Rome marked major stepping stones on Newman's journey towards Catholicism. It was at Rome that they had begun the 'Lyra Apostolica'. This is not at all surprising when one considers the history of Christianity to be found around every corner of the Eternal City: the Vatican itself, which contains the tomb of St Peter, the first pope, the catacombs of the early Christian martyrs that lie beneath, the sculptures of the four early Doctors of the Church that grace the high altar, who were to pay such a major role in the decision of Newman and his fellow Oxford Movement members to enter the Catholic Church, and of course the Church which contains the tomb of the apostle to the gentiles, St Paul outside the Walls. The whole atmosphere in this city at the centre of Christendom puts one in touch with the history of Christianity. As Thomas Merton, the Cistercian monk, wrote: 'It was in Rome that my conception of Christ was formed. It was there I first saw him!'

Prior to Cardinal Newman's canonization, I made a point of going to visit the Propaganda Fide College, and was lucky enough to gain entrance. Winding my way up the beautiful marble staircase and on to a corridor with large paintings of former famous students adorning the walls, I made my way towards the newly restored Newman Chapel. I sensed a very special aura of joy in that beautiful chapel that day — it was the eve of the canonization, and that sense of joy prevailed in the Eternal City throughout the following three days.

FOURTH VISIT TO ROME

When Newman travelled for the last time to Rome in May 1879, the Holy Father had invited him to come in order to honour him by creating him a cardinal. Pope Leo XIII, who had succeeded Pius IX in 1878, had a special affection for Newman and referred to him as *il mio Cardinale*.

> My Cardinal! It was not easy, it was not easy. They said he was too liberal, but I had determined to honour the Church in honouring Newman. I always had a cult for

him. I am proud that I was able to honour such a man.[16]

When Cardinal Newman received the red hat of a cardinal in Rome, the now-famous speech he gave at the ceremony pretty well sums up the primary concern that had occupied him throughout his life since his Oxford days—the spirit of liberalism in religion.

> And I rejoice to say to one great mischief I have from the first opposed myself. For thirty, fifty years I have resisted to the best of my powers the spirit of Liberalism in religion ... [That is] the doctrine that there is no positive truth in religion, but that one creed is as good as another ... It is inconsistent with any recognition of any religion, as true, it teaches that all are to be tolerated, for all are matters of opinion. Revealed religion is not a truth, but a sentiment and a taste; not an objective fact, not miraculous; and it is the right of each individual to make it say just what strikes his fancy.[17]

> Also, I took great pains with what I have published, and am as fierce in my heart now as ever against Liberalism on the one hand and ... extreme (ultramontane) views ... on the other, but it has always been a great pain to me to write.[18]

Notes

1. Newman, *Apologia*.
2. Newman, *Letters and Diaries*, vol. 3, p. 287.
3. Newman, *Apologia*.
4. Newman, *Letters and Diaries*, vol. 3, p. 235
5. *Ibid.*, p. 231
6. *Ibid.*, p. 282.
7. *Ibid.*, vol. 11, p. 253.
8. Newman, *An Essay on the Development of Christian Doctrine*, ch. 1 (p. 45).
9. Newman, *Letters and Diaries*, vol. 13, p. 16.
10. *Ibid.*, vol. 12, p. 23.
11. *Ibid.*, vol. 11, pp. 249–50.
12. *Ibid.*, vol. 12, p. 25.
13. *Ibid.*

14 *Ibid.*, vol. 11, p. 79.
15 *Ibid.*, p. 74
16 *Ibid.*, vol. 29, p. 426, Appendix 1.
17 Newman, *Apologia.*
18 Newman, *Letters and Diaries*, vol. 28, p. 207. I also wish to acknowledge the article on Rome by Dr Brigitte Maria Hoegemann FSO, *John Henry Newman in his Time*, Oxford: Family Publications, 2007, pp. 61–81.

✠ 28 ✠

Rome: Celebration of Canonization

THIS PILGRIMAGE is coming to an end. We are in Rome, where the friends and devotees of the soon-to-be-canonized Blessed John Henry Newman have gathered from all corners of the globe.

The pealing of countless church bells, announcing the Sabbath, breaks the early-morning stillness of the Eternal City. Waiters in starched write aprons arrange tables and chairs outside cafés, with so much diligence and care that one is convinced that theirs is, indeed, the most important job in the world. Aromas of freshly brewed coffee and hot croissants fill the early morning air as I hurry past as the sun is rising over the city.

Oratorian priests, identifiable by their long black cassocks and white collars, make up the largest group gathered in the square. I feel so happy for them, as well as for the different groups of nuns in religious attire, who represent the three new saints from Brazil, Italy and India. The Swiss, some dressed in national Alpine attire, are there to support their new saint, the seamstress Marguerite Bays, a big moment for secular Switzerland!

The crowds that gather in St Peter's Square cannot contain their excitement, and, in some instances, deep emotion, as they are moved to tears. After months and years of persistent prayer and beseeching God for the miracle that eventually happened, the beloved Cardinal Newman is to be raised to the altar of the Church on this special day in Rome.

As I have mentioned before, one has to imagine that the shy, unassuming Newman, who saw the humour in all of life's events, even in the midst of suffering, would be more than slightly bemused at the idea that he is to be declared a saint of the Universal Church. This extremely modest saint really did not believe, as he says, that he was fit to 'black the shoes of the saints'.[1]

But there he surely was. As the canvas with his image was unrolled high on the basilica façade, in the centre of the five soon-to-be-canonized saints, I fancied it portrayed our new saint with a look of surprise, even bewilderment at this honour being bestowed on him.

But St Peter's Basilica—at the heart of the Catholic world—that sits on the place where the first pope and bishop of Rome was martyred, is where St John Henry Newman truly belongs, for he is an exemplary model for those who head the Church in our age. For this saint is a great church leader.

Those who made the pilgrimage to Rome to honour Cardinal Newman were primarily English. The importance that this nation placed on this special event was obvious. The Queen was represented by the presence of her heir, Prince Charles. Other dignitaries included Sergio Mattarella, President of Italy, the Brazilian and Taiwanese Vice-Presidents as well as ministers from Ireland and India. It would have been impossible to count the hundreds of cardinals, bishops and clergy among the 150,000 or so pilgrims that morning.

Melissa Villalobos—the lady whose miracle was responsible for Cardinal Newman's canonization—and her husband and family of seven children from Chicago were all present.

Pope Francis based his homily at the canonization Mass on the Gospel of the day: the lepers whom Jesus heals (Luke 17:19). The Pope concluded:

> Such is the holiness of daily life, which St John Henry Newman described in these words: 'The Christian has a deep, silent, hidden peace, which the world sees not . . .

The Christian is cheerful, easy, kind, gentle, courteous,
candid, unassuming; has no pretence . . . with so little that
is unusual or striking in his bearing, that he may easily
be taken at first sight for an ordinary man.' Let us ask to
be like that, 'kindly lights' amid the encircling gloom.
Jesus, 'stay with me, and then I shall begin to shine as
Thou shinest; so to shine as to be a light to others'.

For the pilgrims gathered in Rome the canonization marked
the high point of a three-day celebration 'filled with a deep
joy' in thanksgiving for the life of John Henry, Cardinal
Newman. This special triduum was introduced with a
celebratory symposium, entitled 'Newman the Prophet:
A Saint for our Times', held at the Angelicum University
on 12 October. The speakers included some of the most
highly esteemed Newman scholars. The Angelicum very
kindly provided an excellent buffet supper at the close of
the lectures.

Afterwards, outside in the darkening evening people
moved *en masse* towards the basilica of St Mary Major, a
short distance away. The great basilica was full to the brim
as the congregation with one voice 'raised the roof' with
a rendering of Cardinal Newman's hymn, 'Praise to the
Holiest', at the opening the Vigil of Prayer.

It is difficult to explain the tangible sense of joyful enthusiasm that filled the great basilica on that eve of the canonization. Suffice to say that it was very special, and that
it occurred to me, not for the first time during those days
in Rome, that something that had long lain dormant in
the English psyche was emerging into the light again — as
the cardinal predicted in his 'Second Spring' sermon. On
this evening Cardinal Newman's own words in this hymn
seemed to make his presence felt.

Cardinal Rylko extended a warm welcome to all, before
the opening prayer was said by the Archbishop of Birmingham, the Most Rev. Bernard Longley:

O God, fount of all holiness, we gather together in joyful
expectation, preparing to celebrate the proclamation

of Blessed John Henry as a saint of your Church. We bring all our prayers and intentions into this church, dedicated to the most holy Mother of your Son, and we ask that they be crowned with her intercession and the prayers of Blessed John Henry Newman.

This prayer was followed by Cardinal Newman's beautiful meditation on trust in God: 'God has created me to do Him some definite service'.

Intercession prayers were led by Melissa Villalobos, the beneficiary of the Newman miracle that had led to his canonization. All voices of the congregation in the packed great basilica joined in singing Cardinal Newman's encouraging words in the hymn, 'Lead Kindly Light', which closes with the beautiful sentiment: 'And with the morn those angel faces smile, which I have loved long since, and lost awhile'.

This memorable evening came to a close with a concert of sacred music sung by the boys of the Schola Cantorum of the London Oratory School with their director, Charles Cole. Impeccably dressed in their choir robes, as always, their truly beautiful and uplifting singing brought this historic evening to a fitting end.

Note

[1]   Ward, *The Life of John Henry Newman*, p. 229.

The Evening of the Canonization

THE ORATORIANS CELEBRATE THEIR NEW SAINT WITH A 'MUSICAL ORATORY'

A SPECIAL CELEBRATION took place on the Sunday evening of the canonization with a 'musical oratory' in honour of this new Oratorian saint, John Henry Newman, at the Roman Oratory Church of Santa Maria in Vallicella (Chiesa Nuova).

When the Oratorian founder, St Philip Neri, first began to gather people around him, they met at first in his room, then in an oratory over the roof of the church at San Girolamo della Carità, and then in a little oratory. The group would discuss prayer and other subjects and some sacred music would be sung to 'refresh the spirits', and prayers would be said. Sometimes these 'oratories' moved outside and took place in the context of a picnic, or a pilgrimage to the seven principal churches.

When St John Henry Newman founded the English Oratory in 1848, he brought to England this form of prayer and music, called a 'musical oratory'. Newman always loved music in the liturgy. On this evening the welcome was extended to all pilgrims gathered in the packed church by the Provost of the Roman Oratory, before 'Praise to the Holiest in the Height' was sung with gusto in praise and thanksgiving for the new saint.

We pilgrims learned a great deal about the life of St Philip Neri that evening, this saint whom John Henry Newman chose to follow and imitate:

> Gain for me the grace of perfect resignation to God's will, of indifference to matters of this world, and a constant sight of Heaven; so that I may never be disappointed at the Divine providences, never desponding, never sad, never fretful; that my countenance may always be open and cheerful, and my words kind and pleasant, as becomes those who, in whatever state of life they are, have the greatest of all goods, the favour of God and the prospect of eternal bliss. Through Christ our Lord. Amen.[1]

This very special day came to a close with the heart-felt singing of the Te Deum in grateful thanks to God for our new saint of the Church.

> Teach me to look at all I see around me after thy pattern as the creatures of God.

> Let me never forget that the same God who made me made the whole world, and all men and all animals that are in it. Gain me the grace to love all God's works for God's sake, and all men for the sake of my Lord and Saviour, who has redeemed them by the Cross. Through Christ our Lord. Amen.

In the afternoon I went with some friends to visit the English College, which had an exhibition exploring St John Henry Newman's four visits to Rome. Newman had visited this college on two occasions on his first visit to Rome.

Note

[1]   The prayers cited here were compiled by the Oratorians for this special 'Musical Oratory'. See also F. W. Faber, *If God be with Us: The Maxims of St Philip Neri*, Leominster: Gracewing, 1994, 2004.

✠ 30 ✠

The Mass of Thanksgiving

NEWMAN DECLARED A NATIONAL TREASURE

O UR TRIDUUM ended with a Pontifical Solemn Mass of Thanksgiving on Monday morning at the papal basilica of St John Lateran, the cathedral of Rome, known as the 'mother of all churches'. The basilica was so crowded that there were more people standing than sitting, and many more outside as well.

Cardinal Vincent Nichols, Archbishop of Westminster, who presided at this special Mass, could hardly contain the joy he felt, he said, 'throughout these wonderful days of deep, deep joy'.

The Irish concelebrants that morning included Philip Boyce, OCD, Bishop Emeritus of Raphoe and Newman scholar, Bishop Fintan Monahan of Killaloe and Bishop Brendan Leahy of Limerick with the diocesan priests Joe Young, Robbie Coffey and Paul Finnerty, and the vice-rector of the Irish College in Rome. The presence of representatives from the Church of England was a reminder of Cardinal Newman's role in Church unity, which was ever close to this saint's heart.

We were here to give thanks for the life of St John Henry Newman and the sentiment expressed in his beautiful hymn 'Praise to the Holiest in the Height' (from *The Dream of Gerontius*) reflected the due praise felt by the huge congregation that filled the basilica to overflowing.

The homily was preached by a bishop of St John Henry's own Oratorian Order, Bishop Robert Byrne of Hexham and Newcastle, who said Newman was a 'national treasure':

> His greatness lies in his intellectual ability to approach the questions of the day from a different angle and a broader perspective. Like his spiritual father St Philip Neri we cannot put Newman in a box; we must let him speak for himself and he will teach us much.

As the Cardinal Archbishop of Westminster led the procession at the end of Mass I counted over twenty-five mitres, representing the bishops from England, Wales and Ireland who were present at the Mass.

✚ 31 ✚

Limerick and Newman

O NE PLACE IN IRELAND that has a very special affinity with John Henry Newman is Limerick. This special link reaches back to that extremely difficult year in Newman's life, 1852, when he was mentally and physically exhausted with the pending Achilli trial and the stress of the difficulties he was encountering in the setting up of his university in Dublin. Newman asked his friend, William Monsell (Lord Emly), an Anglo-Irish landowner who owned a small house at Tervoe, deep in the County Limerick countryside, if he could stay there for a week. Newman stayed at the house in August of that year and it is said that it was here that he completed *Discourses to Mixed Congregations*. 'The quiet set me up. It is the only thing for me ever. I have never been tired of being by myself since I was a boy.'[1]

During Newman's visit to Ireland prior to setting up his university in 1854, when he travelled to many parts of the country to meet with the local bishops, it was Bishop Ryan of Limerick who made the most favourable impression on him: 'He is the cleverest bishop I have met, and certainly to me the kindest'.

The 'Newman Altar' on which he celebrated Mass daily during his time at Tervoe is now located in the parish church of Ballybrown, Patrickswell, Co. Limerick. Newman is still fondly remembered and revered in this parish.

The bishop of Limerick, Dr Brendan Leahy, together with priests from the diocese, led a group of parishioners on pilgrimage to Rome for Newman's canonization.

When the Act of Parliament that integrated Newman's Catholic University into the new combined universities in Ireland became law in 1908, the biggest dissenting voice from among the bishops was that of the then-bishop of Limerick, Dr Edward O'Dwyer.

Note

[1] Letter to Johnson Trevor, Newman, *Letters and Diaries*, vol. 1, p. 609. McRedmond, *Thrown among Strangers*, p. 70.

✝ 32 ✝

The Apologia is Born

N EWMAN'S BRILLIANT SPIRITUAL CLASSIC, *Apologia pro Vita Sua*, was written in response to the well-known Anglican clergyman Charles Kingsley's malicious efforts to harm Newman's reputation in the public mind.

We have previously referred to the difficulties Newman experienced from different sectors of the Oxford community, and further afield, as a result of his decision to enter the Catholic Church, which, he explains, made it impossible for him to remain at Oxford.

Newman had expected that this would happen in the then anti-Catholic England, but he was deeply hurt when family members and some Anglican friends, whom he held in high regard, turned away from him. This really cut Newman to the core, as we note from a letter to William Froude in 1860: 'When I became a Catholic I think I wrote to Rogers to beg his forgiveness if in anything I had acted unkindly to him. My severance from him and others is a wound which will never heal ... The natural heart has wounds as well as the body.'[1]

So Newman was always aware that one day he might be 'called on to defend my honesty while in the Church of England'. Yes, there had been endless attacks but they had been anonymous. But if someone who was well known spoke against him, then he knew he would have to defend his position. He recognized that he had to 'speak strongly', too, otherwise he would not seem to be 'in earnest'.[2]

Thus when Charles Kingsley—whom Newman describes as 'a furious foolish fellow—but he has a name'—launched an attack on him, in essence impugning Newman's honesty, and on the Catholic Church, in a review published in the December 1863 issue of *Macmillan's Magazine*, Newman knew he had to respond.[3] Kingley wrote:

> Truth, for its own sake, had never been a virtue with the Roman clergy. Father Newman informs us that it need not, and, on the whole, ought not to be; that cunning is the weapon which Heaven has given to the saints wherewith to withstand the brute male force of the wicked world which marries and is given in marriage.

Newman responded, protesting to the publishers: 'There is no reference at the foot of the page to any words of mine, much less any quotation from my writings, in justification of this statement'.[4] A long and heated debate ensued through various letters between Newman and Kingsley, which ultimately came to a head on 20 March 1864, when Kingsley published the now famous pamphlet; *What, Then, Does Mr Newman Mean?*[5] Here Kingsley not only repeated the accusation of dishonesty against Newman but expanded on it at length and in depth. An excerpt:

> What Dr Newman teaches is clear at last, and I see now how deeply I have wronged him. So far from thinking truth for its own sake to be no virtue, he considers it a virtue so lofty, as to be unattainable by man, who must therefore, in certain cases, take up with what it is no more than a hyperbole to call lies; and who, if he should be so lucky as to get any truth into his possession, will be wise in 'economizing' the same, and 'dividing it', so giving away a bit here and a bit there, lest he should waste so precious a possession.

From a letter to his good friend Copeland on 31 March 1864, we come to understand how Newman felt the need to respond to such scurrilous accusations of dishonesty and to clear his name in the public arena, but also to defend the Catholic Church:

I am writing my answer to Kingsley's pamphlet... The
whole strength of what he says, as directed rhetorically
to the popular mind, lies in the antecedent prejudice
that I was a Papist while I was an Anglican... the only
way in which I can destroy this, is to give my history
... from 1822 or earlier, down to 1845.[6]

Newman was very reluctant to write this history of his
religious convictions but he wanted to 'tell the truth, and
to leave the matter in God's hands'. He decided he would
write his responses in pamphlets which would be published
on a weekly basis, while the Kingsley controversy was in
the public arena. The first of the eight pamphlets which
would ultimately comprise the *Apologia pro Vita Sua* was
published on 21 April 1864.

From the time he began this work Newman explains
that he was 'writing from morning to night, hardly having
time for my meals'.[7] Never before had any book cost him
so much as this; he suffered a 'stress of brain', but he had
never suffered such 'pain of heart' as well, as he recalled old
friends and family members, who were now departed. He
had been 'constantly in tears, and constantly crying out with
distress'.[8] On one occasion he worked on the manuscript
'for 22 hours running'.[9]

The eight parts or pamphlets were published together
as a single volume in 1864, under the title *Apologia pro Vita
Sua: Being A Reply to a Pamphlet entitled 'What, Then, Does Dr
Newman Mean?'* A second edition appeared the following
year, entitled *History of My Religious Opinions*.

Newman's *Apologia*, which caused him so much stress
and suffering as he struggled to lay bare this personal
account of the history of his religious convictions, is recognized as a great spiritual masterpiece, said to resemble, in
its truth, beauty and clarity, the *Confessions* of Augustine. In
the preface, Newman explains that his one object in writing
this spiritual autobiography was to refute Kingsley's charge
of untruthfulness ('How can I tell that I shall not be the
dupe of some cunning equivocation?') by which Kingsley

had attempted 'to cut the ground from under my foot; to poison by anticipation the public mind against me ... and to infuse into the imagination of my readers, suspicion and mistrust of everything that I may say ... This I call *poisoning the wells*.'[10]

After the publication of the *Apologia*, many of Newman's friends who had turned away from him came back again, having gained a clearer understanding of his religious convictions.[11] Another result was that he won over the affections of the English people, gaining their respect, and this had truly momentous consequences in terms of an acceptance of Catholicism in the country.

Notes

[1]   C. Wilcox (ed.), *John Henry Newman, Spiritual Director, 1845–1890*, New York: Pickwick Publications, 2013, p. 152.

[2]   Newman, *Letters and Diaries*, vol. 21, p. 100.

[3]   *Ibid.*, p. 100.

[4]   Newman, *Letters and Diaries*, vol. 20, pp. 571–2.

[5]   C. Kingsley, *What, Then, Does Mr Newman Mean?*, London: Macmillan, 1864.

[6]   Newman, *Letters and Diaries*, vol. 21, pp. 90-1.

[7]   *Ibid.*, p. 103.

[8]   *Ibid.*, p. 107.

[9]   *Ibid.*, p. 111.

[10]   *Apologia*, p. 6.

[11]   Newman thanked his friends profusely for their support through this ordeal: e.g. Sir John Simeon (10 April 1867, *Letters and Diaries*, vol. 23, p. 140), Isaac Williams (31 March 1865, *ibid.*, vol. 21, pp. 441–2) and W. J. Copeland (letter to M. R. Giberne, *ibid.*, vol. 30, p. 284).

✛ 33 ✛

The Dream of Gerontius

T HROUGHOUT THOSE THREE DAYS IN ROME, we pilgrims
consistently raised our voices in singing those
inspiring and consoling words taken from what
Newman always referred to as 'my own *Gerontius*':

> *Firmly I believe and truly*
> *God is three and God is one;*
> *And I next acknowledge duly*
> *Manhood taken by the Son.*
>
> *And in the garden secretly,*
> *And on the cross on high,*
> *Should teach his brethren and inspire*
> *To suffer and to die.*

The year 1864 had been a trying year for Newman, with the
controversy with Charles Kingsley that ended in Newman
writing his *Apologia*. There had also been his failed attempt
to found an oratory in Oxford. But despite all of this Newman found time to encourage the Catholic convert Fanny
Taylor in her literary efforts.[1]

It was in order to help Miss Taylor find copy for her new
magazine that *The Dream of Gerontius* was first published
in the May and June 1865 issues of her new publication,
The Month.

Newman explains to his friend, T. W. Allies, in a letter
dated 11 October 1865 how at the age of nearly 64 he wrote
Gerontius: 'On the 17th January last it came into my head to
write it. I really cannot tell how, and I wrote on till it was

finished, on small bits of paper. And I could no more write anything else by willing it, than I could fly.'[2] Elsewhere, writing to Lady Charles Thynne, he said it had been 'written by accident—and it was published by accident'.[3]

> As to my own *Gerontius*, it was not the versification which sold it, but the subject. It is a religious subject which appeals strongly to the feelings of everyone. I heard of one farmer who was a most unlikely man to care about poetry, who took to it when he was ill—it was to him a prayer or meditation. It directed his thoughts to the next world, from no merits of its own, but from its subject.[4]

Newman was amazed at the popularity of *Gerontius*, which was an immediate success when published. The poem deals with the journey of a soul from life to death and ultimately to heaven. 'Softly and gently enfolded in the arms' of his guardian angel, to whom the Father gave the soul in charge from his birth 'to rear and train by sorrow and pain . . . from earth to heaven'. The angel's work now done, he brings 'this child of earth' safely to rest 'at the dear feet of Emmanuel'.

The beauty of this dramatic poem could not fail to touch hearts and offer enormous support with its gentle tenderness and understanding to those facing the most dramatic event of their lives.

Frederick Chapman, the editor of Newman's poems, writes of this poem:

> It would seem as though there had been gathered up all the forces that had for so many years been restrained, and the poet . . . shows us, in a sudden blaze of almost intolerable light, the high and awful thoughts that devout meditation and self-suppression have stored up in the mind compounded of reverence and imagination, for which poetic expression was the only natural outlet.[5]

Newman was very touched to hear that it had been used by General Gordon, a Free Churchman, 'in his very last moments' at Khartoum, where he was killed in 1884. He had marked several passages in pencil, such as, for example:

'Pray for me, O my friends; a visitant is knocking his dire summons at my door ... 'Tis death, O loving friends, your prayers!—'tis he! ...: Prepare to meet thy God: Use well the interval ...Now that the hour is come, my fear is fled.'

Gladstone, a devout Anglican, wrote to Newman in 1868, hailing it as 'the most remarkable production in its own very high walk since the unapproachable *Paradiso* of Dante.'[6]

Here speaks the Angel in *Gerontius*:

> SOFTLY *and gently, dearly ransomed soul,*
> *In my most loving arms I now enfold thee,*
> *And, o'er the penal waters, as they roll,*
> *I poise thee, and I lower thee, and hold thee.*
>
> *And carefully I dip thee in the lake,*
> *And thou, without a sob or a resistance,*
> *Dost through the flood thy rapid passage take,*
> *Sinking deep, deeper, into the dim distance.*
>
> *Angels, to whom the willing task is given,*
> *Shall tend, and nurse, and lull thee, as thou liest;*
> *And Masses on the earth and prayers in heaven*
> *Shall aid thee at the Throne of the most Highest.*
>
> *Farewell, but not forever! Brother dear,*
> *Be brave and patient on thy bed of sorrow;*
> *Swiftly shall pass thy night of trial here,*
> *And I will come and wake thee on the morrow.*

Notes

[1] Fanny Margaret Taylor (1832–1900), the daughter of an Anglican clergyman, went to the Crimea as one of Florence Nightingale's nurses, and while there entered the Catholic Church; she later founded a community of nuns, The Poor Servants of the Mother of God.

[2] Newman, *Letters and Diaries*, vol. 22, p. 72.

[3] *Ibid.*, p. 86.

[4] Newman, *Gerontius*, ed. Winterton, p. 5.

[5] *The Poems of John Newman, afterwards Cardinal*, ed. Frederic Chapman. London, John Lane [1905], p. xvii.

[6] Newman, *Letters and Diaries*, vol. 24, p. 7.

✛ 34 ✛

Oxford University Newman Society

I N 1878 THE CATHOLIC GRADUATES AND UNDERGRADUATES
of Oxford established the Catholic Club as a means of
supporting the Church's life within the university. Ten
years later the club adopted its present name, The Oxford
University Newman Society, as a tribute to the memory of
John Henry Cardinal Newman, Oxford's greatest theologian
of modern times. Over the years, the Society has had many
notable members including Gerard Manley Hopkins, J. R.
R. Tolkien and Evelyn Waugh. Today the Newman Society
continues to support the spiritual, intellectual and social
life of the Catholic Church in Oxford University, and in the
wider community of the city itself.

The society provides a focus for Newman's 'friends' to
gather and share. There are Newman Societies in most
major universities in the world today.

✝ 35 ✝

Littlemore College

N EWMAN WROTE, 'as I made Littlemore a place of retirement for myself, so did I offer it to others'.

In the early 1950s the Fathers of the Birmingham Oratory acquired the building in Littlemore, which was falling into ruin at the time, and undertook a complete renovation. With the help of drawings by Newman and his friends it was restored to its original appearance.

In 1987 the everyday care and maintenance of the college was entrusted to the religious congregation, The Spiritual Family the Work, whose approach to what they see as a very precious task is one of great dignity, love and respect. Today Littlemore is preserved as a place of prayer, pilgrimage, retreat and study in the spirit of Newman. There is no mistaking the person who is honoured here, for on entering the garden the first thing one sees is a bust of Cardinal Newman, who dedicated his monastery here to all who visited.

As well as looking after the little chapel, the library and all of Cardinal Newman's memorabilia preserved here, the sisters also look after the constant stream of pilgrims and visitors from all over the world who come here. Talks and meetings are held in the library. Newman's beautiful little oratory, where he spent so much time at prayer, and was received into the Catholic Church, was named as a place of pilgrimage for the Jubilee Year 2000. Many converts choose this as the place to be received into the Catholic Church, as Newman himself was.

During my time at Oxford I often visited the college and the oratory, which has a very special sense of the sacred.

> Arise, Mary, and go take possession of a land which knows thee not. Arise, Mother of God, and with thy thrilling voice, speak to those who labour with child, and are in pain, till the babe of grace leaps within them! Shine on us, dear Lady, with thy bright countenance, like the sun in his strength, O stella matutina, O harbinger of peace, till our year is one perpetual May. From thy sweet eyes, from thy pure smile, from thy majestic brow, let ten thousand influences rain down, not to confound or overwhelm, but to persuade, to win over thine enemies. O Mary, my hope, O Mother undefiled, fulfil to us the promise of this Spring.[1]

Note

[1]   Newman, 'Second Spring'.

✢ 36 ✢

The Ordinariate

WHEN NEWMAN BECAME A CATHOLIC he was followed by a virtual exodus of Anglican clergy, professional men and their families, which caused a huge angst amongst Protestants. In a number of cases whole parishes walked with their Anglican minister to join their local Catholic church. This exodus has been continuing ever since as countless thousands of people have been inspired by Cardinal Newman to enter the One Fold of the Redeemer. A number of young students entered the Catholic Church at the Oratory during my time at Oxford.

An important development in this regard are members of the Personal Ordinariate of Our Lady of Walsingham, established by Pope Benedict XVI on 15 January 2011 in accordance with the apostolic constitution Anglicanorum coetibus within the territory of the Catholic Bishops' Conference of England and Wales.

The Personal Ordinariate is set up in such a way that 'corporate reunion' of former Anglicans with the Catholic Church is possible while also preserving elements of a 'distinctive Anglican patrimony'. The Ordinariate was placed under the title of Our Lady of Walsingham and is under the patronage of St John Henry Cardinal Newman.

The Ordinariate groups and religious communities, which have so far been set up in England and Wales immediately subject to the Holy See, represent an important development in the work of promoting Christian unity, something so dear to the heart of Cardinal Newman.

Conclusion

It has been my misfortune through life, never to have been able to devote myself to one subject in consequence of the urgent calls upon me of the passing hour, so that I have ever been beginning and never ending.[1]

I T WEIGHED UPON NEWMAN that his life had been 'cut up so that I have followed out nothing, and have got just a smattering of many things, and am an authority in none'.[2]

In this new saint we see an extremely courageous man, who dedicated his life to the search for the truth he found in the One Fold of Christ. As we have noted, Newman never allowed the many difficulties and the suffering he experienced to stop him from entering the Catholic Church, or from speaking out when necessary in defence of the Catholics of his age, who were maligned and alienated in the England of his time.

We have noted Newman's generosity of spirit in that he never said 'no' to any request. Hence he found himself bogged down, stressed out and on the verge of collapse on a number of occasions throughout his long life. But he saw every request as a service for God: God has created me to do him some special service'.

It has been said that Newman wanted to be a missionary to help the needy and downtrodden people of the world, but instead accepted that the people he was called to help were those much closer to home.

St John Henry Newman tells us that 'from first to last education has been my line'. Consequently we see him building schools for the children of the then-poor parishes of Littlemore and Birmingham, and a Catholic university in Dublin.

For Newman education was about the formation of the whole person morally and intellectually. Thus he stresses in his university discourses that the formation of the whole person cannot exclude religion.

The sufferings he endured as a result of his decision to enter the Catholic Church were immense. In addition to alienating friends and family members, he was, for instance, stripped of his fellowship of Oriel College, Oxford—this was a cruel blow but he accepted it as part of the price he would have to pay to become a Catholic.

St John Henry Newman's contribution to Ireland is immense; both in his role as the first president of the Catholic University in Dublin, which has grown into University College Dublin, Ireland's largest university, but also in the gift he has left in the beautiful University College Church—Our Lady Seat of Wisdom—on Stephen's Green, Dublin.

Thus students of University College Dublin, past and present, owe a huge debt of gratitude to this English Oratorian priest and distinguished Oxford scholar, who through much research and experience of university life formed the idea of what a university of the highest standard of excellence should be, and went on, despite enormous obstacles, to plant his 'ideal' Catholic university on Irish soil.

I do not agree with those who say his mission to found his Catholic university in Ireland was a failure. One has only to look to what has become the largest university in Ireland today to see how the seed he planted has grown and flourished.

As the history of salvation shows, God has always intervened at critical times for humanity, and has done so by raising up great saints throughout the ages. Pope Benedict said he believed this to be the case, at Cardinal Newman's beatification ceremony.

Newman was specially chosen by God to be a great saint of the Church, who, in the manner of those other two extraordinary converts, St Paul and St Augustine, would lead people back to the One Fold of Christ, at a time, as outlined by Pope Benedict, when there is an 'urgent need' to proclaim the Gospel in the 'highly secularized environment' of Britain and our Western world.

Newman's prophetic vision foresaw many of the problems that have come to pass today. He has been called 'Father of the Second Vatican Council', which recognized the role of the laity in the Church, which was very close to Newman's heart.

His writings confound his critics, and define the authentic doctrines of the Church. 'Truth is passed on not merely by formal teaching, important as that is, but also by the witness of lives lived in integrity, fidelity and holiness.'[3]

Newman repeats his urgent message for our times, over and over again, attesting that the prevailing lies of this age are that there is no positive truth in religion, that any creed is as good as any other. When he received his cardinal's red hat it was not surprising that he reiterated the teaching he felt so strongly about in relation to the spirit of liberalism in religion:

> And I rejoice to say to one great mischief I have from the first opposed myself. For thirty, fifty years I have resisted to the best of my powers the spirit of Liberalism in religion ... [That is] the doctrine that there is no positive truth in religion, but that one creed is as good as another ... It is inconsistent with any recognition of any religion, as true, it teaches that all are to be tolerated, for all are matters of opinion. Revealed religion is not a truth, but a sentiment and a taste; not an objective fact, not miraculous; and it is the right of each individual to make it say just what strikes his fancy.[4]

Conclusion

The following beautiful prayer tells of Cardinal Newman's hope and trust in God throughout his life and of his appreciation for all that God has done for him:

> O my God, my whole life has been a course of mercies and blessings shown to one who has been most unworthy of them. I require no faith, for I have had a long experience, as to Thy providence towards me. Year after year Thou hast carried me on—removed dangers from my path—recovered me, recruited me, refreshed me, borne with me, directed me, sustained me. O forsake me not when my strength has failed me. And Thou never wilt forsake me. I may securely repose upon Thee. Thou wilt still and to the end be superabundantly true to me.[5]

We conclude our pilgrim journey in the footprints of St John Henry Newman with his words ever accompanying us:

> O hope of the pilgrim! Lead us still as thou hast led; in the dark night, across the bleak wilderness, guide us on to our Lord Jesus, guide us home.

Notes

[1]   Newman, *Letters and Diaries*, vol. 33, p. 30.
[2]   *Ibid.*, vol. 19, p. 508.
[3]   Newman, *Apologia*.
[4]   *Ibid.*
[5]   Newman, *Meditations and Devotions*, p. 367.

BIBLIOGRAPHY

Bertram, J., *Newman's Oxford. The Places and Buildings Associated with John Henry Newman during his Years in Oxford 1816–1846*. Leominster: Gracewing, 2019.

Boyce, P., OCD, *At Prayer with John Henry Newman*. Rome: International Centre of Newman Friends, 2007.

— *Mary: The Virgin Mary in the Life and Writings of John Henry Newman*. Leominster: Gracewing, 2001.

Chesterton, G. K., *The Victorian Age in Literature*. London, H. Holt & Co, 1913.

Cockshut, A. O. J., 'The Literary and Historical Significance of the "Present Position of Catholics"', in *Newman after a Hundred Years*, ed. I. Ker and A. G. Hill. Oxford: Clarendon Press, pp. 111–27.

Faber, F. W., *Growth in Holiness. The Progress of the Spiritual Life*. London, 1855.

Hoegemann, Sr Brigitte Maria, 'Newman and Rome', in *John Henry Newman and his Time*, ed. P. Lefebvre and C. Mason. Oxford: Family Publications, 2007, pp. 61–81.

Iglesias, T., 'Why did Newman come to Dublin?', *The Irish Catholic*, 10 October 2019.

Kelly, S., *A Conservative at Heart. The Political and Social Thought of John Henry Newman*. Dublin: The Columba Press, 2012.

Ker, I., *John Henry Newman, A Biography*. Oxford: Oxford University Press, 1990.

— *The Achievements of John Henry Newman*. Edinburgh: T. & T. Clark, 1991.

— and T. Merrigan, *The Cambridge Companion to John Henry Newman*. Cambridge: Cambridge University Press, 2009.

McCartney, D., *UCD — A National Idea, The History of University College Dublin*. Dublin: Gill & Macmillan, 1999.

McRedmond, L., *Thrown among Strangers, John Henry Newman in Ireland*. Dublin: Veritas, 1990.

Monahan, F., *Newman — Saint for Our Time, A Perfect Peace*. Dublin: Veritas, 2019.

Newman, J. H., *Apologia pro Vita Sua*. London: Penguin Books, 1994.

— *Autobiographical Writings*. London and New York: Sheed & Ward, 1956.

—*Certain Difficulties Felt by Anglicans in Catholic Teaching Considered in Twelve Lectures Addressed in 1850 to the Party of the Religious Movement of 1833*. London: Longmans, Green & Co., 1901.

—*The Dream of Gerontius, The Month*, May and June, 1865; later editions, ed. M. F. Egan, London: Longmans, Green & Co., 1903; ed. Rev. G. Winterton, Leominster: Gracewing, 2013.

—*An Essay in Aid of a Grammar of Assent*. London: Longmans, Green & Co., 1903.

—*An Essay on the Development of Christian Doctrine*. London: James Toovey, 1845 ; later edition ed. J. Tolhurst, Leominster: Gracewing, 2018.

—*Fifteen Sermons Preached before the University of Oxford*. London: Longmans, Green & Co., 1909.

—*Historical Sketches*, 3 vols. London: Longmans, Green & Co., 1908–9.

—*The Idea of a University; Defined and Illustrated*. London: Longmans, Green & Co., 1902.

—*The Idea of a University; Defined and Illustrated*, ed. D. M. O'Connell. Chicago: Loyola University Press, 1927.

—'The Infidelity of the Future', in *Catholic Sermons*. London: Burns & Oates, 1958.

—*Lectures on the Doctrine of Justification*. London: Longmans, Green and Co., 1908.

—*Lectures on the Present Position of Catholics in England, Addressed to the Brothers of the Oratory in the Summer of 1851*. London: Longmans, Green and Co., 1908 ; later edition ed. A. Nash, Leominster: Gracewing, 2000.

—*The Letters and Diaries of John Henry Newman*, ed. C. S. Dessain. 32 vols. Oxford: Oxford University Press, 1961–2008.

—*The Life of John Henry Cardinal Newman, Based on his Private Journals and Correspondence*, ed. Wilfred Ward. London: Longmans, Green & Co., 1912.

—*Loss and Gain: The Story of a Convert*. London: Burns & Oates, 1881; later edition ed. S. Gilley, Leominster: Gracewing, 2014.

—*Meditations and Devotions*. London: Longmans, Green & Co., 1907.

—*My Campaign in Ireland*. Aberdeen: King, 1896; later edition ed. P. Shrimpton, Leominster: Gracewing, 2020.

—*Parochial and Plain Sermons*, 8 vols. London: Longmans, Green & Co., 1907–8.

—*The Poems of John Henry Newman*, ed. F. Chapman. Sacred Treasury series. London: John Lane, 1905.

Bibliography

—'Second Spring', in *Sermons Preached on Various Occasions*. London: Longmans, Green & Co., 1908 ; later edition ed. J. Tolhurst, Leominster: Gracewing, 2008.

—*Sermons bearing on Subjects of the Day*. London: Longmans, Green & Co., 1902.

—*University Teaching Considered in Nine Discourses*. London: Burns, Oates & Washbourne, 1908.

—*Verses on Various Occasions*. London: Longmans, Green & Co., 1890.

O'Faolain, S., *Newman's Way*. London: Longmans, Green & Co., 1952.

O'Loughlin, T. *Cardinal Newman, Seeker of Truth*. Dublin: Veritas, 1988.

Shrimpton, P., *The 'Making of Men'. The Idea and Reality of Newman's University in Oxford and Dublin*. Leominster: Gracewing, 2014.

Sugg, J., *Snapdragon in the Wall: The Story of John Henry Newman*. Leominster: Gracewing, 2002.

Van de Weyer, R., and P. Saunders, *I Step, I Mount, The Vision of John Henry Newman*. London: Lamp Press, 1950.

Ward, M., *Young Mr. Newman*. London: Sheed & Ward, 1948.

Ward, W., The Life of John Henry Newman, based on his Privated Journals and Correspondence. London: Longmans, Green & Co., 1912.

Winterton, Rev. G., *The Dream of Gerontius*. Leominster: Gracewing, 2013.

9 780852 447604